PRESENT-DAY TRENDS
IN RELIGIOUS EDUCATION

Lectures on the Earl Foundation
and Other Papers

ERWIN L. SHAVER

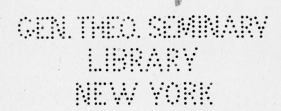
THE PILGRIM PRESS

BOSTON   CHICAGO

Copyright, 1928
Sydney A. Weston

MADE IN U. S. A.

Dedicated
To the Memory of
My Father

INTRODUCTION

The purpose of this volume is indicated in the title. The comparatively recent movement to take religious education seriously in our churches is beset with all the problems which any youthful individual or institution faces. It is lively and energetic and there are those who would repress it. It is enthusiastic and "rushes in where angels fear to tread," sometimes declaring that the pastor's work is nothing but that of religiously educating! It would save the world, often unmindful of the fact that the world is not saved by methods alone, and occasionally needing the advice "physician, heal thyself." It is misunderstood, even when it is earnestly seeking to make its best contribution to the building of the kingdom of God.

It would be more than presumptuous, however, for one to attempt to explain to those who may not be in the "inner circle" of religious educators all the problems of modern religious education and what the various leaders are trying to do about them. For the inner circle is not entirely agreed as to purposes and methods. But there are questions which ministers, laymen and even religious educators are rightly asking which should receive an answer. A few of these are treated in this book. An examination of the chapter headings and sub-headings in the Table of Contents will show that a number of the more puzzling questions are squarely faced. It is sincerely hoped that

the discussions will be informative and thought-provoking to those who are honestly seeking to understand present-day trends in religious education.

The material for approximately one-half of the
volume consists of lectures delivered by the author on
the Earl Foundation at the Pastoral Conference held
under the auspices of the Pacific School of Religion
at Berkeley, California, in 1926. The remainder of
the volume includes articles published in religious
education journals and also considerable unpublished
material. All of these have been carefully revised
and organized so as to give up-to-date and unified
treatment to the subject. The author acknowledges
with appreciation the courtesy of the *Elementary
Magazine* for the privilege of reprinting an article
which he originally prepared for this publication and
which furnishes the larger part of the second chapter.
Likewise, he acknowledges the use of articles written
for the *International Journal of Religious Education*
and *The Westminster Leader* which he has used as
portions of the final chapter.

ERWIN L. SHAVER

Boston, Massachusetts
    June, 1928

CONTENTS

CHAPTER ONE

EDUCATIONAL PROBLEMS OF TODAY

One is tempted to begin a discussion of such a subject as our chapter heading implies by quoting statistics showing the extent of what has been popularly called "spiritual illiteracy." We must grant the fact that twenty-seven millions of children and youth without any connection with a church or synagogue in America should cause a religious educator to do some profound thinking. The reader, we believe, is sufficiently impressed by what he has heard and observed regarding this condition so that we move on beyond the fact to what would seem to be more fundamental. We should ask ourselves in the light of such a state of affairs: "Can it be that these millions are outside religious influences because they have not been instructed in the Bible? Or are not both of these facts related to each other, not as cause and effect, but as concomitant symptoms of more complex and underlying difficulties?" We cannot rest our plea for more and better religious education on statistics alone.

Or again, one might list some of the more apparent and much discussed evils of the present day, characterized as departures from the high standards of individual and social morality of our forefathers' days.

We would prefer to take our stand, if side we must, with those who say in reply, as did the Preacher long centuries ago: "Say not that the former days were better than these, for thou dost not inquire wisely concerning this." But on the other hand, we must honestly admit that there are many things that are not right in the life of today, and the religious educator cannot pass them by in blind optimism or with the sand-founded faith that this generation will automatically sow its wild oats and move on to higher levels of living. We are willing to grant most of what the critics may say about individual and social sins. We reserve the right, however, to insist that we will have to go still deeper, if we are to find the roots of the matter.

Extending our range still further out upon the world horizon, we watch with fascination and yet with serious concern the great drama of international relations, as political, commercial and scientific events afford a stage setting far beyond the wildest imaginings of the most prophetic of our forebears. One cannot refrain from saying, although it is trite: Surely we are in one of those periods of transition which are the milestones of civilization's progress. The twentieth century movement of the nations was most picturesquely described a few years ago by General Smuts of South Africa, when he said: "Humanity has struck its tents and is once more on the march." The figure is exceedingly revealing.

Since the world situation is bringing to religious

education at the present time its most pressing problems, it may be well to note certain facts which will
serve as a background for our later discussion. The
first of these is the growth of national and racial
consciousness on the part of every section of humanity, especially in the case of those groups which feel
that they have been oppressed and deprived of their
rights. This applies also to the so-called "backward
nations." They are demanding equality of opportunity, a "place in the sun," the right to make their
contribution—whatever it may be—to the sum total
of world good. There is therefore a strong consciousness of nationalism and racial integrity and the
attempt by every possible means to arouse and
strengthen the national and racial morale.

The second fact, which it is well to take account
of, is that of the shrinking of the globe upon which
we live, figuratively speaking. The picture is well
drawn in a four sectioned cartoon which appeared
last year in a Chicago newspaper. In each section
was a sketch of the globe, with the size decreasing in
the order of reading and with the water divisions
becoming narrower and narrower until in the last the
oceans separating the continents were mere rivulets.
Missions, trade, exploration, travel for pleasure,
science and invention—each has added in recent years
large contributions toward making the world one
neighborhood. Isolation, even though we were to
agree upon its desirability, is possible only by turning
backward the hands of the clock of time. We must,

by the very expressions of the divine urges within us, live together as races and nations. And with this fact there come a host of new and difficult problems centering about the question of just how we shall relate ourselves one to the other in this interdependent world.

Science, too, has facts we must notice. Psychology, for example, has busied itself among other things with the measurement of human intelligence, the inborn, untutored capacity of individuals and races to acquire and apply knowledge. The substance of comparative studies of the abilities of various national and racial groups is that, with incidental exceptions, they are essentially on a par. And this fact is one which these groups are beginning to realize and to use to their advantage.

A fourth fact, which we should particularly study as educators in the field of religion, has to do with the principles whereby the nations and races of the earth have related themselves to one another in the distant and immediate past. There was a time, which seems to be passing, when "might made right"—the "mailed fist" principle, by which the physically stronger clan, tribe, nation or race lorded it over those whom it could terrorize by military force. We are a bit ashamed of this principle now; at least we are unwilling to boast of it as we once did. In its place has come another, which receives more hearty approval, the principle of "wisdom gives the right to rule," the "clever mind" principle, by which the nation with the most efficient government justifies its procedure of imposing its domination over the weaker and more ignorant groups of mankind. But Christian thinkers are beginning to question even this less objectionable principle on the grounds of the ulterior motives of the governors and the ineffectiveness of a "hot-house" method of teaching the weaker nations how to govern themselves. They say that we must move on to adopt a third principle, that of mutual appreciation and cooperative service, which is the law and spirit of Jesus' teaching for individuals and nations alike.

Pressing as these objective needs—spiritual illiteracy, low standards of morality and the problems of international and inter-racial adjustment—may be, nevertheless, our problem as Christian educators is concerned primarily with certain objectives and means in our program of training children, youth and adults. There are many factors which need analysis and attention in our present programs, both in the field of general education and of religious education. As typical background materials for the remaining chapters of this volume, however, we shall select only four. These four, we believe, are sufficiently representative and important for treatment in this chapter as showing the strategic opportunity of Christian education and the necessity for its being carried forward on the highest level.

EDUCATION FOR MATERIAL GAIN

In bygone generations the outstanding goal of education was cultural, the making of a well informed man. The past few decades have seen a transition from this aim to that of developing a person who is economically efficient. This vocational, or "bread-and-butter," aim of education is the product of various causal factors. The natural desire to have an education produce tangible results, the pattern set for us by industrial education in other countries, our own rise and stupendous growth in material prosperity, the commercial and financial supremacy which came to us during the war and the additional buttressing of a naturally consequent pragmatic philosophy—all these have tended to strengthen our faith in the validity of this objective for education.

It has found expression up and down our educational ladder. The child in the grades finds the commercial emphasis in geography and arithmetic; his older brother finds the pursuits of the newly organized Junior High School especially designed to fit him for a vocation (that is, manual labor); or if he perchance go further, he may attend a separately housed commercial or technical High School, an institution unknown to our forefathers; the older children in the family may choose between a variety of colleges, but more and more likely are they to select one which fits them for some niche in the world of commerce. A most interesting sidelight upon the college situation in this respect is found in the recent statement by one of the world's richest men that students in our colleges ought to pay in tuition the entire cost of their education, because they are intending to choose money-making as their profession, whereas endowed colleges had originally been established to provide cheap education to such servants of humanity as ministers and teachers.

What are the outcomes of this increasing emphasis upon the vocational aim in education? We note such as these: A man's worth is measured in terms of his income; individuals can converse only about their own "line"; efficiency and production become the twin gods of national life; the motto of business is "do the other fellow before he does you"; the competitive spirit governs the manufacture and production of goods, irrespective of economic waste. Commerce tends to color all the other aspects of our life. Our art, our music, and our recreation are entangled with money-making schemes. Our health is in the hands of those who have foodstuffs to sell. Our science is asked to state a price for its services. Our governmental policies are threatened by billion-dollar corporations. Even our religion must be organized upon a basis of efficiency and its Founder's greatest qualities center about his executive ability!

On the other hand, there are bright spots in the picture. The tendencies we have listed are but general and all humanity is not asleep. There are doctors who refuse to sell their healing formulae to food and drug corporations for exploitation. There are business men who foresee the day of mutual cooperation in ownership and labor in the fields of manufacture and commerce and have bent their energies to find the best ways of bringing it about. There are thinkers who are putting us in contact with other civilizations where the dollar is not worshiped and we are learning that life is not all bread. There is an unorganized but none the less real youth movement which sees more friendly relations between races and nations. There is still that within us which thrills, not only at the heroism which drove a young man to cross the wide Atlantic alone in his airship, but in the integrity of life purpose which enabled him to refuse to barter his popularity for gold.

Here, then, is a real task for Christian education—to change the now dominant objective of our educational program from that of fitting the child merely to become an efficient producer of goods into an objective of service, not in the popular commercial meaning of the term, but in the light of the example of Him who "came not to be ministered unto but to minister."

EDUCATION FOR NATIONALISM

A little less than a century and a quarter ago the little kingdom of Prussia passed a compulsory education law which was designed to inculcate in its rising generation a love of fatherland and which it hoped would be a very powerful factor in making the nation great and especially effective in time of crisis. For

Prussia had just been forced by Napoleon to sign a very humiliating treaty and the sting of defeat was still felt keenly. It seems that her statesmen had for more than a generation been thinking about some means whereby they could strengthen the national morale and finally hit upon the use of a state controlled system of education. Heretofore education had been viewed as a purely private affair. But now, for the first time in modern history, we see it employed as an instrument to forge out such a type of national idealism as the nation desired. The man placed in charge of that system of state schools was first called a commissioner of education; but within ten years, so well did the plan work, he was raised to the rank of a minister, equal in standing to all the other ministers who sat in the king's privy council and advised him.

If the moving picture camera had been used in the past to record memorable scenes and we could unroll the reels which described an event in the city of Paris in the year 1870, here is what we would see: A triumphant army marching down its beautiful boulevards with a great general riding at its head. And if we could hear him speak, this is what we would hear: "Behold the triumph of the Prussian—school master!"

If we could also review a certain scene in Berlin in the year 1890 we would see a great gathering of the schoolmasters of the German Empire assembled at the command of the newly crowned Emperor, William II, as one of the first acts of his reign. And we would hear him exhort them to be true to the trust which was theirs as moulders of the nation's destiny. It was their first duty, he argued, to teach unswerving loyalty to the ideals of the nation as its rulers had decreed—and so on. The results of this policy of education for nationalism we find in the war of 1914 and the years which followed.

One is not to assume, however, that we are holding up a single people as an example in a critical spirit. We are trying to show that education as a tool of the state had shown its effectiveness. Other nations, slowly but surely, saw the efficacy of the new tool, more powerful than artillery or battleships. France, embittered by the defeat of 1870, turned to compulsory education in 1881 to instill into her growing citizens a loyalty which would meet any test. England, where education had never been a neglected institution, in the zero hour of her destiny in 1918, passed the Fisher Act, thereby doing more for education than she had ever done in her history.

Our own country, having left education together with other unmentioned powers to the several states, has in recent years been forced, by the immigration to our shores of millions of foreign birth and ideals, to find ways of teaching Americanism. There have been many agencies established to develop an abiding loyalty to the ideals of our democracy. So strong has the feeling become that there have been frequent bills proposing to establish a secretaryship of education in the president's cabinet and to distribute as a subsidy one hundred million dollars to aid education in the various states. America, too, is quite aware of the results which can be obtained in the way of national loyalty through the instrumentality of state-controlled education.

As we note the progress which is being made in those countries which are now having a renaissance of national spirit, we see that they also are committed to education for nationalism. The examples of the Western nations have not passed unnoticed by those of the East. China, Japan and Turkey are shining examples. Russia, Mexico and the countries of South America alike are forging ahead. Some nations are spending far more than we, in proportion to their total budget, for this purpose. In fact there is not a nation of even the slightest standing on the face of the earth which is not making vigorous use of education as a means of teaching loyalty to its particular ideals.

We can thus see that here we have to reckon with a new factor in seeking to bring about harmony in the world. Whether the nationalism being taught in each case is sufficiently broad to allow for the growth of the brotherhood spirit remains to be seen. It may be the nationalism of the "mailed fist," or the nationalism of the "clever mind," or, if Christian education can make its vital contribution, the nationalism which includes the whole world in one vast brotherhood.

PSEUDO-EDUCATIONAL METHODS

A third problematic factor in the educational situation today is the tendency to develop and to utilize certain methods of changing the minds of both old and young which are of doubtful educational worth. Two perfectly good words among others have been taken over to identify these pseudo-educational procedures—namely, "propaganda" and "promotion." This does not mean that all which goes on under these terms is necessarily bad, but so much of it is that the words have come to signify approaches to education which by no means reflect its highest levels. Curiously enough, each of the objectives we have been discussing has been a contributing factor in lowering educational standards. From the materialistic emphasis we get the use of the word "promotion" as applied to the development of interest in business enterprises. From the nationalistic emphasis we secure the word "propaganda" as applied to the means of fostering love of one country to the exclusion of others. The use of the low level type of education involved in these practices has been made possible by the application of certain psychological laws to the conduct of business and war and to other aspects of social life as well. Since propaganda and promotion methods produce the results desired by those who use them, their employment in a materialistic and nationalistic civilization has become quite universal in recent years. The true educator needs to study their use and proceed to counteract their influence by the highest type of educational procedure.

We may point out a few of the many evidences of

the wide-spread use of these methods. We are, of course, quite familiar with the efforts which were put forth to produce a closed mind with regard to anything German during the war, irrespective of the truth of the facts involved. Our very governmental agencies were organized to sow the seeds of hatred. The production emphasis in our commercial age has not only made use of advertising to inform the public of the goods available, but by applying psychology to advertising, it has actually created new demands quite irrespective of the need of the purchaser and the fact that many other concerns had products "just as good" or even better to meet legitimate needs. The advertiser, through the use of psychology, can manipulate at will the law of supply and demand and is doing thereby the very thing which he warns us about in his arguments against socialistic schemes. Given money enough to employ persons skilfully trained in the use of psychology in creating public opinion and to purchase space for his propaganda, one can make the people buy whatever he has to sell or believe his views with regard to almost any subject.

Any prominent educator in the field of general education will tell you that one of his greatest troubles is to keep his school free from the influence of some-one with an ax to grind. It may be the manufacturer of some "health" product, the agent of the Society for the Relief of Suffering Billy Goats, the "one hundred per cent American" disturbed about bolshevism being taught in the schools, or the zealous

Bibliolatrist who despairs of Christianity's being able to win men freely to follow the way of Jesus and wants the children compelled by law to know the Bible. The child is easily exploited and there are many who want to use him to their selfish ends.

The church, too, is not free from the charge of having lowered its standards to make use of such non-educational procedures as we are discussing. It has followed business and other agencies in the employment of the ad writer and the publicity expert. It has mobilized executive secretaries and organized for promotion. It has allied itself with this and that worldly agency and in diplomatical fashion sought to arouse sentiment wholesale in favor of its wares. In fact, practically every agency, good as well as bad, is tempted to seize upon these pseudo-educational instruments which promise to bring quick returns.

May we here point out in brief summary fashion the failures of such methods from the standpoint of true education: They are based upon the theory that the end justifies the means; they tend to disregard the whole truth; they appeal to the emotions rather than to the rational mind; they make use of haste because they are interested in immediate results and know that the reaction will come sooner or later; they coerce by appealing to the mob mind; they put their trust in organization rather than in the willing spirits of the organized; they want to "pass a law" to compel their way; they are perfectly satisfied with a competitive theory of social organization; they believe in the rightness of the majority vote, after they have brought the majority to their way—these are a few of the many indictments which may be brought against the use of such so-called educational procedures which fail to educate thoroughly. It is the task and the privilege of Christian training agencies to lead the way in insisting upon a type of education which is free from these defects.

INSTITUTIONALIZING EDUCATION

Another tendency which is characteristic of procedures in education today is that of turning over to institutions the training responsibilities which rightly belong to parents. On every hand we hear public school authorities, church educational leaders, workers for various child character-training and welfare agencies and others interested saying: "The home no longer teaches the children; therefore we (who represent the school, the church or other agency) must do it." Someone has paraphrased the ancient scripture to read: "When my father and mother forsake me, the Boy Scouts will take me up." The paraphrase ought not to allow us to think that the Scout agency is the only such rescue agency, for we have many institutions ready to take over the work which parents have laid down.

There are, of course, many reasons why this has come about. Doubtless we will find that the educational factors we have been discussing in this chapter are underlying causes. Keeping these in mind and looking at the situation from the angle of the parents, we easily see that they find the institutional care very efficient, that it gives them certain ease and freedom from responsibility, that they do not have the specialized training for many of the modern educational techniques, and that it is more convenient to ask another to train a child in a way of life which our own practice makes it inconsistent to talk about.

It does not take extensive research into the workings of our present organized public school system, for example, to see what is happening. The school year has steadily lengthened. A large number of public educators have pronounced themselves in favor of a twelve months school year. The school day has also lengthened. If we consider the control which the public school exercises over the time of the pupil outside of the building in supervising both his study evenings and his extra-curricular activities, we can see that the actual school day is longer than we had supposed. Add to these facts the gradual tendency to raise the compulsory attendance age limit in various states. Note, also, that the latest type of education being experimented with is the "nursery school" and recall how the kindergarten began as a private affair only to be incorporated into the public system. On every hand we see the steady growth of the control of a public institution over the time of the child's life. But we must look even further. The public school, like others, was formerly looked upon as a mind-training agency. Today it has taken over the body of the child through its programs of supervised play and health education. And tomorrow, without a doubt, for we already see the signs, the public school will direct the moral or character development of children. It would begin to appear that before long this institution of public creation is to be responsible, not only for the child from his toddling days until complete maturity, but for his training in every phase of life activity.

We have not the space here to go into the fact that there is an increasing number of other institutions likewise seeking to relieve us of the responsibility for the training of our children. The number is growing and considerable competition between them is developing. Nor can we exclude the church from the list. To a certain extent, religious educators also are substituting various schools, such as the Sunday school, the week-day school and the vacation school, to say nothing of many other appended societies and clubs, for the work which should, in part at least, be done by parents fellowshiping in the home and in other places with their children.

The evils always attendant upon mass education; the failure to take account of individual differences; the withdrawal of education from the activities of everyday life; the ignorance, indifference and actual helplessness of parents who do not understand the mysteries of the technically trained educator, general or religious; the further pushing of the home into the background of oblivion—all these are consequences of institutionalizing education. We must find ways to remedy this situation. Parents must resume their responsibility in cooperation with public and private school teachers, with religious educators and with others who assist in guiding and protecting children. The school, or place where education actually takes place, must come to be viewed as involving the home, the farm, the workshop, the playground, private and public, the church and other places wherever older folk are working and playing—and in the school, in this sense of the term, there will be many teachers, including every parent and every adult who controls the experiences which the normal child ought to have. But we cannot do this by turning over the child to an institution with four walls and a corps of highly trained and even fine charactered specialists to do our work for us.

In this task of freeing education from institutionalism, which will involve training parents as associate teachers and many other new plans and methods which we cannot discuss here, Christian education has the needed approach and dynamic in the principles and practice of Jesus. To be true to these, it should be willing to sacrifice even its own life that all that is best in education shall be preserved.

Here, then, are a few of the educational needs of the new day: the reconstruction of objectives so that materialism and nationalism shall be replaced by spiritual idealism and world-wide love; the reconstruction of means so that pseudo-educational pro-

cedure shall give way to methods which are consistent
with those high goals; and the reconstruction of our
agencies so that the home has its rightful place once
more and we resist the subtle temptations of institutionalism. Here is no small program for the combined efforts of all educators. Blessed be those who
call themselves religious educators after the manner
of Jesus, if they humbly lead the way.

FOR FURTHER STUDY

ATHEARN, WALTER S. *Character Building in a Democracy.*
Pilgrim Press.

COE, GEORGE A. *Law and Freedom in the School.* University
of Chicago Press.

COE, GEORGE A. "Religious Education and Political Conscience,"
Religious Education, volume XVII, pages 430-35.

COE, GEORGE A. *What Ails Our Youth?* Scribner.

FLEMING, DANIEL J. *Whither Bound in Missions?* Association
Press.

KILPATRICK, WILLIAM H. *Education for a Changing Civilization.* Macmillan.

MARTIN, EVERETT D. *The Meaning of a Liberal Education.*
Norton.

McGIFFERT, ARTHUR C. "A Teaching Church," *Religious Education,* volume XVI, pages 3-9.

REISNER, EDWARD. *Nationalism and Education Since 1789.*
Macmillan.

ROBINSON, JAMES H. *The Mind in the Making.* Harper.

WEIGLE, LUTHER A. *The Training of Children in the Christian
Family.* Pilgrim Press.

WEIGLE, LUTHER A. *et al. The Teaching Work of the Church.*
Association Press.

Chapter Two

THE NEW RELIGIOUS EDUCATION

In order to meet the educational needs of the new day, such as we have pointed out in our first chapter, leaders in religious education have been developing new ideals and procedures. An understanding of the nature of these new purposes and practices depends upon our recognizing many facts. Some of these facts have been directly presented and others indirectly implied in our discussion thus far. Three factors which are necessary to form an intelligible background for the points we wish to present in this chapter are: (a) the Christian purpose for mankind, (b) the laws of educational psychology which tell us the nature of child life and the ways in which Christian character may be developed, and (c) the present world situation in which children must live and be taught. It is not within the scope of this volume to treat the first two of these factors, except as incidental deductions with regard to them are found necessary to the discussion. Assuming that the reader has a working understanding of these two points, we wish to survey briefly a few of the problems involved in the third factor and then proceed to set forth some of the more significant trends in present-day religious education as they are revealed in the thought and practice of forward-looking leaders.

Let us first take stock of the world situation in which children are living today. We gather such facts as these: The geographical world is shrinking with amazing rapidity. The events of every bit of the earth's territory are at once the common property of every other section of the globe and its people— men, women and little children. This fact raises scores of problems with regard to the training of immature persons which were unknown to the educators of past generations. The world of today is also a very complex world. It is a world of speed, of tremendous organization, of multitudes of social movements, of conflicting and of "entanglingly allied" social ideals, all of which make clear thinking and the discovery and practice of right courses of action extremely difficult for adults, to say nothing of children.

Again, for the first time in history, the truth is now clearly seen that the universe is run according to law. Religion, which at first opposed the idea, has finally accepted it as a fact. The more difficult problem, however, has yet to be solved—namely, how religion may and must use the laws of science to further its great enterprise. This dawning of a scientific era has thus raised, not only the question of the reinterpretation of the meaning of God and religion, but the staggering responsibility for going far beyond mere intellectual reconciliation into the realm of the positive and passionate activity which are implied in its acceptance.

Into the world of today there has also come a deeper and deeper penetration of the spirit of democracy. Much as we have found it difficult to make democracy work and in discouragement have fallen back upon the services of some form of dictatorship in the recurring cycles of history, we cannot entirely rid the human mind of the notion that it offers the only right way to relate ourselves one to another. The passing generation has observed the democratization of the relations between men and women. The present is faced with the "revolt of youth" which in one sense is a fact. The "divine right" of parents to rule their children must be succeeded by the divine right to love them, and the problems of this new relationship must be worked out to a successful solution even though at great cost.

Finally, as we take an inventory of the world situation, we note with a sense of mingled pride and shrinking that it is a world which has high ideals. We are tempted to become pessimists when we hear and see about us evidences of evil which amount (so it seems) to almost a tidal wave. But is it not that we viewed these things more complacently in previous periods of history or ostrich-like refused to admit their existence? Is not a sense of sin after all a good thing, the forerunner of a religious reformation? Let us discover (that is, admit the existence of) more and more sin and sharpen our consciences until we raise humanity to a higher level of living. And this we must do not only for ourselves but for our children's sakes. How hard it thus becomes in the present hour to teach our children to live on a plane loftier than that upon which we or others before us have yet lived!

This world, then, with its problems of "rubbing elbows" nation with nation, of complex social organization, of scientific law, of extending democracy and of higher ideals, is a world to be mastered, a world to be used and a world to be enjoyed. Into this world comes the child of today. If what the psychologists tell us is correct, and we see no reason to doubt them, he comes with the same native equipment that the child of fifty thousand years ago had with which to begin life. His raw materials, from which he must make a life of purpose and usefulness, consist of the same instincts and urges, the same degree of activity, the same peculiar traits and capacities. It would be nice, perhaps, to think that human nature could transmit by the process of reproduction the things it had learned in one generation to its heirs in the next. But the best we can do is to transmit, by a social heredity, the heritages of a better environment, of a more efficient method and of a loftier purpose. And the fine thing about it all is the fact that it pays great tribute to the power of education. Each generation has thus been able to lift its children speedily from crude, instinctive activities, expressed without purpose to be either religious or irreligious, to activities which represented a more and more Christian way of living and challenged the self-satisfied ways of the past.

Our task, then, as Christian educators is to help our children face the facts of the world of today and master the technique of living on the Christian level. And by Christian level we mean, not the level of the days of baptism by the sword, of armed feudalism, of trial by ordeal, of the debtor's prison, of human slavery, of infant damnation, or of the legalized sale of alcoholic beverages, but the level of a new day in which we find a way to end war, to bring about industrial democracy, and to practice friendship between the races of mankind. The way in which our leaders in the field of religious education are proceeding to bring in the new day is shown by such educational ideals as these:

MAKING RELIGIOUS EDUCATION INTERESTING

Religious education is and should be viewed by children as an interesting process. Religious educators, like others, have long been under the thralldom of the disciplinary theory by which learning was supposed to be of necessity largely a process of endurance of uninteresting subjects. But with a new psychology and a clearer view of Christianity, we believe that children will gladly put forth their best energies if their religious education is rightly planned. The monotonous drill upon the questions and answers of the catechism which no child could understand has step by step given way to a process of giving the child an experience of religion by living it, doing those things which are within his powers of comprehension and ability and which lead him on to the things which are before. Think of the new features which gladden the hearts of children in our more modern church schools: the beautiful rooms and equipment; the music which appeals not to the lower, but to the higher emotions; the workshops and gymnasiums; the countless service projects undertaken which have to do with actually helping someone who is flesh and blood; the class and departmental organizations with their practice of democratic self-government; the extension of the training program into the week day; the increasing opportunities to take a real part in the worship life of the church. Children now are going to church school, not because they must, nor because there are prizes to be given out, but because they like it and their life interests are being met.

RELIGION CONCERNS ALL LIFE

Religious education is a re-interpretation of all life. The very kind of world we described at the opening of our discussion is abundant evidence that religion, if it ministers to the needs of the twentieth century, must come out of its compartment and help children meet their problems of daily living. That is just what is happening at the present time. It means for religious education a wide variety of courses and topics. It means some real mental struggles for children and for their teachers as well. It raises the question of how much of the curriculum should be a direct study of the Bible for its own sake. Certainly a part of the courses should be based upon the child's everyday needs and include enterprises to be carried through by him to help in and learn about the building of the Kingdom of God. Hence we find in our progressive schools classes of children discussing and acting upon, with guidance from the teachings of Jesus and other Bible characters, their play problems, their duties in the home circle, their relations to community and national government, their treatment of near and distant peoples of other races, the care of their bodies, their use of money, their treatment of friends, and similar questions without end. Nothing that concerns the issues which children meet is escaping from the curriculum of religious education.

RELIGIOUS EXPERIENCE MUST BE COMPLETE

The child has a right to a complete experience of religion. One reason why the older revivalistic appeal has been discredited in seeking to train children in religion is the fact that its appeal was too exclusively to the emotions, and the effect was not lasting. We are in danger just now of making our approach to the child's life too exclusively through the intellect. So we find our better schools recognizing the fact that the child expresses himself not only through his emotions and through his mind, but also through his bodily activities. The training process, therefore, should include thoughtful study and discussion; appreciational training, re-creation through play and through programs of worship; and many "things to do" with the hands and feet, which we popularly speak of as service activities. We cannot list details of these programs here, but we must say that these various forms of religious experience should be naturally related to each other. For example, the themes for children's prayers ought to be found naturally in their study, play and service enterprises. In these ways the child becomes a Christian through-and-through; he thinks as a Christian, he has definite Christian sets and attitudes, and he habitually makes the Christian response as a "doer of the Word." We wish we could say that most of our church schools were realizing this need for a complete experience of discipleship with Jesus, but there are enough who have caught the vision to encourage us to say that the rest will follow soon.

CHRISTIAN CHARACTER A BY-PRODUCT

Self-development and world reconstruction are one process. As we have advanced in our methods of teaching the way of Jesus to little children, we have noted that the materials for the lessons have had to be found in real work which the church was doing. In order to actually "form habits as they will be used," as one Christian psychologist puts it, we have had to enlist boys and girls in the very kind and quality of friendly service which their older friends are undertaking. In fact, we have asked them to take over such portions of the program of making a more Christian world as are within their powers of understanding, of appreciation and of strength of body. So it has come about that learning to be a Christian and being a Christian are one and the same process. Children grow in Christian character as they assist in making Jesus' kind of world. Many leaders are testifying to the joy which their children express when they engage in projects which are just as thrilling to their hearts as the adults' enterprises are to them. Character thus becomes, not something to be priggishly sought for in Pharisaic manner, but a wholesome and unconscious "by-product" as Jesus meant it to be.

PREPARATION COMES THROUGH PRESENT EXPERIENCES

The path to the future lies through the present in the child's religious education. For many centuries we have tried to make the child a grown-up, either by expecting him to be dressed and trained in manners as an adult or by expecting him to have an adult view of religion. Now we are becoming more patient and we realize that it takes at least two decades to make a man out of a child and that one of the key qualities of a teacher of religion is patient waiting. It is well to keep in mind the kind of man we want him to be; but it is well to be satisfied with each short step that he takes. If he can learn to play fair with his companions on the playground; be courteous and kind to his parents, to his teachers and to his friends; joyously enter upon a simple service enterprise such as sending

a doll to an orphanage; pray in language of a little
child, but withal in true faith; learn a few of the facts
about and in the Book of Books—if he can do these
things as a child of his age and experience should,
then we may rest satisfied that he will be able to enter
upon experiences just a little more advanced in the
spirit and way of Jesus and finally come to the more
perfect stature of an adult Christian.   Church-school
leaders today are committed to this principle of the
gradual enrichment of the experience of becoming a
Christian, although the details of method are not yet
completely worked out in practice.

Science Reveals God's Method

Religious education needs science—that is, it needs
both the techniques of science and the mastery of them
in the service of the Christian enterprise.   An illustration of this fact in the work of one teacher shows the
possibilities in every school.   A teacher of nine-year-
olds was discovered with a minature geological exhibit
which she and her class had been collecting.   There
were rocks of various kinds, petrified leaves and wood,
shells, and a toy model of a dinosaur!   But these were
not the only source materials.   Questions brought out
the fact that by judicious use of the Bible and this
little exhibit the children were getting not only an
understanding of how this earth had come to be what
it is, but also a thorough appreciation of the fact that
"in the beginning God" was present and that it was
His way which science was revealing.   There will be

no conflict between religion and science for these children in their later years, for "God's in his heaven: all's well with the world." We are just at the beginning of an era when science is to be accepted as giving the method of cooperating with God, and religion is to furnish the purpose and motive for helping Him.

THE PARTNERSHIP SPIRIT

The child is a junior partner in the Christian enterprise. Steadily we have been taking children into our confidence and companionship in the church. Instead of showing a paternalistic attitude and talking down in childish fashion, we act toward them in the light of what they may be, even as we believe God takes an attitude of faith toward us. This does not mean that we expect adult standards of achievement, but that we recognize that the essential nature of democracy consists, not in the fact that all are equal in talents or abilities, but that all are to be treated as if they were. It is only in this spirit, for which Jesus is sponsor, that true religious education can be attained. We see the beginnings of this in the programs of a few churches. The children's sermon, which we wish might be placed in the setting of a truly "family worship service"; the occasions when even young children take over church services and present ideas in various forms for adult consideration; the "all-church" play times; the mission projects in which every group in the local church has a hand—such as these show practices and possibilities for children and adults expressing the higher form of Christian brotherhood in their mutual relations.

EXPERIMENTING IN HIGHER LIVING

Religious education must be experimental to a high degree. It is not enough to teach children how to live according to the standards of today. Nor is it enough to depend too much upon the experience of the past for standards of action. Though the Bible may give us exemplary ways of living which are very helpful, it likewise contains ideals which must be experimented with, because no one has ever taken them seriously. Therefore we find forward-looking teachers seeking to have their children act as Christians toward peoples of other races and religions and undertaking rather daring projects of world friendship, so daring that older people often criticise. But it is only as this kind of experience enters into the religious education of little children that they will know how to live tomorrow as God wants them to live. For, somehow, we have faith that the people of tomorrow will see face to face what we see now only darkly, even as we have seen some ways of expressing Jesus' love which our forefathers did not discern.

There are many problems to be met before the ideals we have described for the religious education of the children of today are fulfilled. The reader has doubtless expressed many of them involuntarily as he has been reading. But in conclusion we may select two present-day tendencies for particular mention. One is the danger of over-attention with respect to children. We have too many agencies all trying to do the same thing with them and often the child is dragged hither and thither to keep a program going. Have we not forgotten our first purpose to actually help children? There is a real danger of over-stimulation and the development of an introspective attitude.

Another problem is that of forcing children to live more and more in an adult world. As we stated in the begining, what adults experience children are, by the nature of things, experiencing also. How to shield them from some experiences and how to introduce them to others in such a way that they can be helped by them is yet to be discovered. The way out here lies in two directions. We ourselves must be converted from the errors of many of our adult ways and we must also develop a consciousness of a Christian community life which, while it is "in the world," is not "of the world." We must formulate and carefully supervise those experiences suitable for Christian children apart from the selfish forces of evil. For

"The child heart is so shy a thing;
   A look may startle or may charm;
   A passing word may soothe or harm;
The child heart is so shy a thing.

"The child heart is so shy a thing;
   It opens at love's tender call;
   It closes when fear's shadows fall;
The child heart is so shy a thing."
                     —*Anon.*

FOR FURTHER STUDY

BETTS, GEORGE H. *The New Program of Religious Education*. Abingdon Press.

CASE, ADELAIDE T. *Liberal Christianity and Religious Education*. Macmillan.

COE, GEORGE A. *A Social Theory of Religious Education*. Scribner.

COPE, HENRY F. *Organizing the Church School*. Doran.

FISKE, GEORGE W. *Purpose in Teaching Religion*. Abingdon Press.

HARTSHORNE, HUGH. *Childhood and Character*. Pilgrim Press.

MYERS, A. J. W. *What is Religious Education?* National Sunday School Union (London).

SOARES, THEODORE G. *Religious Education*. University of Chicago Press.

SHAVER, ERWIN L. *The Project Principle in Religious Education*. University of Chicago Press.

WEIGLE, LUTHER A. *et al*. *The Teaching Work of the Church*. Association Press.

CHAPTER THREE

A NEW APPROACH TO METHOD

The Christian church, in extending its influence and perpetuating its own life, has used various means to produce in prospective members a vital experience of the meaning of the Christian life. In the generations immediately past, and to some extent at the present time, the process has been largely concerned with an appeal to the emotions. In fact, one can still recall revival meetings in which the convert who was considered to have the most enviable religious experience was the one whose ecstasy led him into a state of trance. This emotional emphasis is rapidly disappearing; in fact, it would seem that the most desirable religious experience in some localities is one entirely devoid of emotional glow. One must say it to the credit of those who fostered the appeal through the emotions that they were seeking to produce an experience which reached to the inner depth of life. The fact that the experience lost much of its apparent vitality because it was too exclusively emotional we must admit. But the sincere purpose to produce in the individual, adult or child, an experience which would result in effective Christian living is to be commended.

At the present time we seem to be on the crest of

another wave, that of instruction. We are seeking to make Christians by an appeal to the intellect. In fact, the terms religious education and religious instruction are almost universally synonymous. To be sure, we have worship programs which are supposed to arouse the higher feelings, but, being crowded with discussion, with emphasis on technique, and subordinated to the all important "lesson" period, they lose a large portion of their potential effectiveness. One could give many evidences of our present faith in instruction as the almost exclusive way in which immature Christians are to be made into effectual citizens of the kingdom. Our curriculum is a series of textbooks containing bodies of information; our methods consist in "getting the truth over" into the mind of the student; our reliance is upon the lesson hour, whether it be on Sunday or in the newly discovered opportunity of the week day; our new architecture lays great stress upon the classroom atmosphere; and there seems to be an increasing tendency to turn the training of our young over to professional character mentors instead of giving ourselves as older friends in true character-making fellowship.

IMPROVING THE INSTRUCTIONAL EMPHASIS

All this is said, however, with the reservation that there have been forces at work to improve the instructional emphasis. One way is the endeavor to have the learner make an imaginary application of the truth or principle of the lesson to his own life. Through the use of stories supplementing the Bible account, the introduction of illustrative materials such as models, curios and the like, the use of pictures to make more vivid the facts of the lesson, and the witnessing of plays and pageants with their dramatic appeal, instruction on the catechetical level or of the textbook memorization type has been somewhat improved. Then, too, the socialized recitation and the discussion method have gone far to connect the theme of the lesson with the problems of the pupils and assist in transfer from classroom to daily life. But the process, in spite of all these improvements, is still one of intellectual approach.

Another type of procedure which has been introduced for the purpose of getting ideas to function in life and guarantee Christian conduct has been the use of expressional activities. The theory upon which these have been initiated is the familiar phrase, "no impression without expression." In general, these expressional activities are of three kinds. One kind consists of handwork. On its lowest level, handwork has been known as "busy" work and as such has had practically no value in church schools. On higher levels, handwork has taken the form of coloring verses and pictures, clay modeling, map making, dramatizing and the like. In all these activities the theory is, in most cases, that the physical activity of the hand and other portions of the body helps to make the idea a part of the whole life of the pupil and insures living in the way implied in the aim of the lesson. This has often reached absurd lengths. For example, one is teaching the lesson of Jesus and the woman who touched the hem of his garment; the handwork suggested is that of having the children take a square of cloth and with needle and thread sew a hem around the edges. Or in another case the lesson is treated of Jesus walking on the Sea of Galilee. The expressional activity is to have the children line up in a row, move their hands after the fashion of sailors rowing a boat and sing "Heave ho, my lads, heave ho."

At the present time another type of "expression" is also prominent. This is the use of the term as applying to the pupil's verbal testimony as to what he thinks about the various truths he has been taught. Those who use the term in this sense speak of the morning Sunday school as the time of "impression" and the young people's society as the "expressional" meeting. While one can discover obvious values in meetings in which freely offered testimony and discussion are abundant, it is plain that talking about the Christian life falls somewhat short of being complete expression of that life.

A third type of activity which has been introduced into the religious education program to assist in vitalizing instruction is the addition of a service program. In this we come much nearer an experience which reaches out and beyond the intellectual approach and affects the physical habits of the becoming Christian. Says Weigle: "The only true preparation for life is life itself; the only effective training for service is to

serve. . . . In the moral and spiritual realm there is
no genuine expression save that of deeds."[1]   We must
grant the effectiveness of a properly directed service
program in any church school.   One difficulty arises,
however, when we try to correlate it with a program
of instruction and worship and find an essential unity
for the whole.

A SEARCH FOR A RICHER EXPERIENCE

Thus it is seen that up to the present time religious
education has failed to discover a procedure by which
it could produce a religious experience on the Christian
level which would at one and the same time affect
the learner's entire life organism, intellect, emotions,
and bodily reactions.   Of this search for such an
experience Coe said several years ago: "Anyone who
has followed intelligently the struggles of the last
quarter-century to develop pupil activity in the church
school knows that there is the central problem of
method in the teaching of religion, and that as yet
this problem is only partly solved in either theory or
practise.   'Home-work,' 'hand-work,' 'expressional
activities'—these familiar terms represent a genuine
digging at the difficulty, but this digging has not
reached the bottom.   All of us are sure that the
process that effectively educates is activity evoked in
the pupil, but we do not know how to discover the
activities that are most educative, or if they were dis-

[1] *The Pilgrim Training Course,* First Year, p. 163.

covered how to evoke them."[1] In this statement he
suggested that the direction in which we are to find
the solution of our problem lies in two factors, an
experience which involves activity of body and heart
as well as head, and one which the pupil will enter
upon gladly because its point of departure is found
in his natural interests.

The Project Principle

It is to meet these difficulties, and a number of
others at present facing religious educators, that the
project principle of teaching is offered. While at first
thought it may appear to be a new procedure, it has
its roots far back in the experience of the race. The
best teachers of all ages have used it to a greater or
less extent. Jesus was a Master indeed at teaching
of this character, as we shall point out later. The
term "project" came into use in connection with
laboratory work in science and agriculture about two
decades ago. Since then, it has been taken over into
other phases of education, its principles have been
more clearly defined and a considerable body of experience with its use has been accumulated. It will be
noted that we have spoken of it as the project *principle*
rather than the project method. One reason for this
is that it is not so much a competitive method in contrast to the various techniques of teaching now
employed as it is the introduction of a somewhat revo-

[1] *Teaching Adolescents in the Church School* (Shaver), p. vii.

lutionary, and yet ancient, procedure, in the use of which all these other methods are usable and necessary. Again, it places much emphasis upon a number of other concepts which are receiving the support of modern educators so that it is a synthetic and all-inclusive approach to the learning process.

We shall begin our interpretation of project teaching by taking up its central concept, which as we have suggested, is the emphasis upon learning through purposeful activity. Children, young people, and even adults learn to live, not so much by discussing theoretical principles about life as by practising living. We learn to do by doing; we learn to love by loving; we develop a Christian character by a series of experiences in the practice of the Way. We must not infer, however, that by the use of the term activity only *physical* action is meant. Rather, we think of the learner reacting as a unitary organism to the situation he faces. He is making certain physical reactions, but at the same time new ideas are coming to him and there are appropriate emotional responses.

CHANGES IN GENERAL EDUCATION METHOD

May we first illustrate the principle by noting a few of the changes which have taken place in recent years in the teaching of the common school subjects. As we have said, the project idea was first used in science and agriculture. Likewise, most newer subjects, unhampered by traditional methods, have been taught in this manner. Witness the manual arts of woodworking, sewing and cooking; the commercial subjects—typing, bookkeeping and stenography. Take the case, however, of such a subject as learning to spell. We can remember lesson after lesson in spelling based on some central theme. Sometimes it was the use of a Latin or Greek root; the dictionary was thoroughly explored to discover all the possible words that were derivatives of that root, with scant regard to their use in the daily life of children, or adults for that matter. Technical words, obsolete words, words used only occasionally in a lifetime, were all included. Spelling books were compiled upon categories of logic rather than psychology. The writer recalls to this day a lesson in spelling on "the crimes," in which the word m-a-y-h-e-m appeared. He has tested numerous audiences of Sunday school teachers and ministers and only here or there can we find individuals who know its meaning. But spelling is changing. The words which children and adults use most frequently and which are most commonly misspelled make up the lessons. Pupils often have their own individual lessons, drilling upon words which they have found difficult to master. Therefore, we have "spelling scales" and lists of "spelling demons" in place of the categorically arranged books of former days.

Or, take the subject of geography. In days past geography was a dry-as-dust subject, taught in question and answer fashion. How we labored to memorize names of oceans, bays, capes, capitals, rivers, and what not! But this has changed. The principles of man's relation to the earth upon which he lives are discovered by an examination of the geographical features of the pupil's own neighborhood. The subject is also made interesting and life-like in various ways. I recall that about two years ago, stepping into the street from my office, I ran squarely upon two urchins of foreign extraction with their hands full of colored folders. "Where did you get those?" I questioned with a guess as to their nature. "At the Tours office around the corner," they replied. "Going to take a trip to Europe in geography, aren't you?" I ventured. "Yes, sir!" And then, after a pause, as if reflecting, the older of the two said, "My father didn't have a chance to go to school until he was eighteen years old." What was in the lad's mind as a background to that statement? The fact that school was an interesting and enjoyable place to be and that he was going to make the most of his chance. This is borne out by the testimony of two truant officers who retired from the Boston school force some time ago. They told the "enquiring reporter" that children like to go to school these days and that parental ignorance and economic necessity were the major causes of truancy.

If we had time, we might speak of changes in the teaching of arithmetic, reading, grammar, and other subjects. But all these represent the public school at work upon the task of developing specific skills or knowledges in growing youth. In addition to the age-old cultural aim and the present vocational, or bread-and-butter, aim of the school, a new goal is being set up; namely, the citizenship or development-of-personality aim. The public school, for example, is more and more seeking to produce the good American citizen, the man who possesses the ideal American character. It is the school in this phase of its activity which gives us the largest insight into procedures which are adaptable to religious education.

The New Approach to Citizenship Training

The subject, if we may speak of it as a "subject," which is designed to do this, is civics. More and more Americanization, or character training in accord with American ideals, is being thought of as a by-product, but nevertheless the most important product of all teaching which goes on in the school. I recall an hour spent with Superintendent Wirt of the Gary schools several years ago. We began by talking about the work of the week-day schools of religion in his community. Our conversation shifted to the subject of citizenship training. He informed me that he had been criticized by certain educators who held to the direct method of character education on the ground that he did not have enough courses on "How to be a Good American." He then proceeded to spread out before me the reports of the activities of the Gary schools; activities for adults as well as children; activities of a wide variety—athletics, dramatics, socials, classes, lectures, musical performances and many others—in all of which the pupil-participation element is strong. "Now," he said, "I believe that there is citizenship education in all of these. Wherever a new American comes in contact with an American of longer standing, Americanization takes place." This view represents, also, the attitude of that most interesting educator, Angelo Patri, and practically all leading schoolmasters of today.

Let us turn our attention, however, to civics as a single subject in the curriculum of the public school and note the changes which have taken place. In the early periods of the development of our schools there was no subject corresponding to what we now know as civics. Whatever citizenship values were obtained came through a study of American history. Then came a period when attention was paid to memorizing the constitution, or constitutions, federal and state, supplementing the study of history. Next it became a separate study and was dignified by having its own books and recitation periods, but still with emphasis placed upon memorization. Later came books in which the stress was laid not so much upon memory of articles and clauses as upon the explanatory text material. But today we are finding quite a new procedure, of which we shall give a typical example.

In a suburb of a large eastern city, the chairman of the city zoning commission wished a map of the city made for the use of the commission. This would cost, if prepared by adult surveyors, several hundred dollars. This chairman conceived the idea of having the high school civics class do the work. Both the class and the instructor were eager to take over the job and they set to work. They surveyed and recorded the various types of living quarters in the city, the stores and factories, the public buildings and parks, the garages, the barns, the chicken coops and the rabbit hutches. Even the gateman's shanty at the railroad crossing was not overlooked. Each of these was represented on the completed map by its appropriate colored sticker, cut in a certain fashion. The work was more accurate than that which adult professional surveyors would have produced. The children worked at the surveying outside school hours. They forgot the movies and their games; they even skipped their lunches; their parents could not get them to go to bed, so eager were they to carry out their project. They talked zoning everywhere; the business men heard them on the streets and the parents in the homes. The result was that they learned more facts, not only about zoning but about all phases of civic life, than if they had been studying out of a book. They learned who the city officials were and whether they were good or bad; they learned about fire and police protection, about sanitation and health, about trade and industry, about elections and countless other facts and principles of American government. And they not only learned facts and principles, but they practised the art of living as good Americans, for were they not making a real contribution to the life of the community and doing, as they expressed it, "our duty to our city"?

This is but one illustration of the new approach to civic education. One could tell of Junior Red Cross societies, of safety clubs, of parliamentary meetings, of health pageants, of school gardens, of clean-up campaigns and of civic tours. All these are expressions of the project idea as it applies to developing, through eager and active participation in worthwhile enterprises, not only a knowledge of essential facts, but definite and thoughtful habits of living as good citizens, with the whole experience suffused with the warm glow of patriotic devotion. Many educators have assured us that this is the only way to develop a desired character or its constituent elements. Says Dewey, "There is nothing in the nature of ideas *about* morality, of information *about* honesty, or purity, or kindliness, which automatically transmutes such ideas into good character or good conduct."[1] We have a similar statement from the late Dr. Gulick, the apostle of play—"Habits of conduct cannot be inculcated by right instruction. Right living is not transmitted by telling children to be honest and true and brave. It is developed in the individual as a phase of other activities and through the example of parents and other adults, working, playing and carrying on their social life together with the children."[2] Jane Addams gives us this statement: "If these young people who are subjected to varied religious instruction are also stirred to action, or rather, if the instruction is given

[1] *The Moral Principles of Education*, p. 1.
[2] *A Philosophy of Play*, p. 219.

validity because it is attached to conduct, then it may
be comparatively easy to bring about certain social
reforms so sorely needed in our industrial cities.   We
are at times obliged to admit, however, that both the
school and the church have failed to perform this office, and are indicted by the young people themselves."[3]

Jesus' Training Program

We have already spoken of the fact that Jesus'
training program was of a project character.   An
examination of his procedure in the training of the
twelve, which we will all grant was his outstanding
educational work, reveals methods quite different from
our attempts at character education.   Jesus had
neither classrooms, nor books, nor equipment.   He
held no formal classes.   He did not cover his material
in any prearranged and logical order.   He gave no
memory work and set no examinations in our meaning of the term.   But day after day, as he and his
disciples passed along the highway or down the village
street, they found people in need.   Here the need was
physical, here mental, here a matter of faith.   While
he applied himself to the renewing of life, his disciples
looked on as observer-students in training.   At first
they assisted in the minor details; later they were
given an opportunity to go out two by two to practise;
finally they were given the entire task with the promise, "Greater things than these shall ye do."   Often

[3] *The Spirit of Youth and the City Streets*, p. 159.

the day's experience included happenings of other types. At times it was a social event which they attended; at times it was the sight of a beautiful field of ripening grain, of children at play, or of laborers at work. But whatever happened became for Jesus the occasion for a lesson. No prearranged lectures, textbooks, or recitations kept him from using every experience as it occurred to teach some portion of the principles of his better way of life. He had, it is true, some great objectives, such as brotherhood, love of truth, respect for personality and reverence for the Father. It was through each day's life, however, that these were to be taught, not through books or words. He did talk to his disciples, but his words were interpretations of the experiences through which they were passing. We have taken these interpretations and tried to make them live by keeping them in their original setting. It is very doubtful whether Jesus, were he on earth today in the flesh, would use these experiences of two thousand years ago to illustrate the great principles of life. He would find in the countless activities and relationships of modern life sufficient material for educative experiences, by which he could make his principles plain to his followers.

FOR FURTHER STUDY

BRANOM, MENDEL E. *The Project Method in Education.* Badger.

COE, GEORGE A. *Law and Freedom in the School.* University of Chicago Press.

DEWEY, JOHN. *Democracy and Education.* Macmillan.

Dewey, John. *Moral Principles in Education.* Houghton Mifflin.

Hosic, J. F. and Chase, S. E. *Brief Guide to the Project Method.* World Book Co.

Kilpatrick, William H. *Foundations of Method.* Macmillan.

Kilpatrick, William H. *The Project Method* (Pamphlet). Teachers College.

McMurry, Charles A. *Teaching by Projects.* Macmillan.

Stevenson, J. A. *The Project Method of Teaching.* Macmillan.

Whipple, Guy M. (editor) *Twentieth Yearbook of the National Society for the Study of Education,* Part I.   Public School Publishing Co.

See also reference list at conclusion of the following chapter.

Chapter Four

A NEW APPROACH TO METHOD (*Concluded*)

Thus far, we have confined our attention to the concept which we have said is central in project teaching —namely, that of learning through purposeful activity. It is now our intention to take up three other qualifying factors which are determinative of good project teaching. As we do so, we shall endeavor to give a number of examples of religious education projects which have been carried on in church schools. Although these illustrations may be given to clarify the factor we are then discussing, it must be kept in mind that, to a greater or less extent, they are illustrative of all the factors involved in the project principle, and particularly the central idea of learning by doing.

Learning Is in Proportion to Interest

The first of these factors is that of interest. The importance of this element, which Kilpatrick has called "wholehearted purpose," is scarcely secondary to that of activity itself. When the disciplinary theory of education was dominant, learning was thought to take place only to the degree to which the subject being studied was hard and disagreeable. Now we hold the reverse and say that real, purposeful effort will be put forth and the experience will be educative to the extent to which the learner finds in it the expression of his natural interests. If he can find it an outlet for his physical, mental and emotional energy, so that all else is forgotten and there is no need for threats of punishment or sugar-coated prizes, then he has identified himself with the experience so intensively that it will remain with him and act as a life-influencing lesson.

Let us take an illustration. In a certain vacation school, it was planned to have the pupils make furniture and equipment for the new parish house to be built the following year. In the course of the school, the boys made a variety of things, such as vases, offering baskets, tables, curtains, bulletin boards, and play equipment for the kindergarten. As the work progressed, "the difficulty arose, not in getting the groups to come for these sessions, but to prevent them from 'living' at the church day and night!" As one of the boys was sandpapering the bulletin board which was to be placed in the rear of the church, he was overheard to remark: "Say, it'll be great when I am a man and come walking into church to point to this board and say, 'I helped to make that, when I was a kid.'" And the girls sometimes cannot refrain from saying, as the offering is taken, "They are using *our* baskets." In this church both children and adults have come to appreciate their mutual contributions to its life. Such a project suggests that habits of church loyalty are not developed by intellectual or emotional appeals, but by a deeper experience in which all the energies of children can find whole-hearted expression.

Interest in valentines was made the point of contact in a project carried out by a second-year primary class, which decided to send "A Message of Love to Mrs. ....," their superintendent. This message of love, they decided after discussion, should take the form of concrete deeds of service which they could perform for her. Each child contributed one, written on a heart-shaped piece of paper, and then all were bound together with red covers. The following are the messages in which they pledged themselves to be more helpful:

I will pay attention. Hughie.
I will not throw chairs around. Charles.
I will pick up scrap papers. Mildred.
I will not destroy material which others wish to use. Angie.
I will not poke or punch my neighbor during the worship hour. Arthur.
I will try to be always on time Sunday morning. Ann.
I will try harder to learn the songs. Frank.
I will not be late. Annie.
I will remember to bring what I promised. Dickie.
I will try to bring a new member for my class. Mary.
I will close my eyes, bow my head, and keep silent during prayer. Austin.
I will be a gentleman at all times. Robert.
I can and will help with the singing. John.
I want to be of service to everyone. Helen.

While visiting an intermediate department some time ago, I came upon a box of marbles upon a table. My

nature are legion and should act as an incentive to
church-school leaders.

We are finding similar constructive projects in progressive church schools. For example, the senior department of a Boston church decided to work out a
Christmas pageant, which should be, not merely the
rehearsal of the ideas of some prominent pageant
writer, but their own creation. They began in the fall
to write one with three episodes entitled "The Prince
of Peace"—Episode I, In Old Testament Times; Episode II, The Birth of Jesus; and Episode III, In the
Life of Today. The preparation of the material became the study activities of three classes, one studying
Old Testament, one studying New Testament and the
third studying the problems of modern social service,
missions and international friendship. Their pageant
was presented the Sunday evening before Christmas to
their older friends as a message or sermon, with the
suggestion that it be treated as such, rather than as an
exhibition to be applauded. Although it may not have
been perfect from the standpoint of the dramatic critic,
these young people received a real Christian experience
in thus making a contribution of a creative nature to
the program of their church.

Some years ago, a class of high school boys in a
rural village more than a mile from a railroad station
undertook the project of furnishing their church with
a weekly calendar. The idea grew out of the fact that
the superintendent gave the class an old hand power
printing press to do with as they pleased. With two

meetings a week, taking down and setting up forms, they gained not only an elementary knowledge of printing, a familiarity with hymns, quotations and scripture passages, and many an hour of wholesome recreation, all under the leadership of a Christian teacher, but they developed the very vivid consciousness of having a significant share in the ongoing life of the church.

A class of junior boys and girls began a study of the work of the American Missionary Association when they discovered that neither they nor their parents knew anything about this society. They corresponded with boards at headquarters, with the missionary schools and the individual scholars. They searched yearbooks, reports and magazines, and sent presents to their new-found friends at Christmas. As the year advanced, they were asked to take over a mid-week service and tell the church members what they had found. Their program included short papers, explanation of prepared charts and posters, a dialogue and testimonies as to what the entire project had meant to the class. Among other things, their testimony stressed the fact that boys and girls in the church school could do worth-while things for their church.

COOPERATION AIDS THE LEARNING PROCESS

A third factor which is necessary for effective teaching of the project type is co-operative work. The socialized class of the public school has its counterpart

in organized group activity in the church school.   It is
certainly highly Christian that the emphasis upon co-
laboring as "many members in one body" should find
expression in the teaching process of the church.   This
spirit of co-operation should be evident not only in the
relations between pupil and pupil but between the
teacher and the pupils and, as we have implied,
between the class and other groups in the total church
life, the community and the world.   In the place of a
learning process which viewed the individual scholar
as an isolated unit, we must substitute a learning
process in which the individual finds his best educational self-realization in the progress which is made
by the groups, large and small, of which he is a member.   We will give two illustrations.

A class of junior boys and girls, just before Thanksgiving, expressed a desire to sell things at the bazaar
which their mothers were holding to earn money for
the old people's home.   The far-sighted teacher
welcomed the idea, but gave it a somewhat different
turn.   She suggested that it might be nice for the class
to pay a visit to the home and sing for the old people.
Accordingly two Saturdays and a Sunday session inter-
vening were spent in preparing the following program:

Introduction: "Why we have come to the Home."—F.
Hymn: "Come ye thankful people, come."
Prayer of Thanksgiving—written by C.
Our Hymn of Thanks: "We gather together to seek
    the Lord's blessing."
Psalm 100—memorized for use on this occasion.

"The Story of the First Thanksgiving"—a poem written by C. F.

Hymn: "America the Beautiful."

The poem was first prepared in prose form, but one of the girls was not satisfied and her poetic skill produced the final form. The children wrote the prayer, drilled themselves upon the psalm, practiced hymns, dressed lolly-pops (!) as favors, packed baskets of fruits, and prepared Thanksgiving cards with verses. Many were the evidences of the co-operative spirit. One boy was overheard to caution the others: "Count the lolly-pops. We want to have enough for them all. Don't want to miss any of the old people. It would be terrible if we have only seventy or sixty-nine and there are seventy-two old people. Terrible to be short two or three. Can't we have a few extras to be sure to have enough?" And again: "We ought to know that psalm better to repeat it without the book." So two of the boys went into a corner with their Bibles and drilled. At the Saturday lunch it was discovered that but one girl could say grace. The discussion led to an awakening of interest in this subject and a list of things they were thankful for was placed on the board. Following the happy experience of singing for the old people, they discussed the fact that they had felt very close to God in their service, searched their Bibles for passages appropriate to the idea and decided, at the suggestion of one of their own number, to make a prayer of thanks which each member of the class might use on Thanksgiving Day in his own home.

Another project with a marked degree of group co-operation took place in a senior department of high school girls. The girls had decided to spend the year in making a series of story books, entitled "Heroines of Service," as reading matter for a school of colored children in the South. After studying a home mission textbook as a background, they set to work. In the course of the year, a number of unexpected sub-projects arose. They decided to have "a real live intellectual Negro" speak to them at their local girls' conference. When his church burned to the ground the very week of the conference, they voted to outfit a girls' dressing room in the new building which was planned. They searched diligently and were finally successful in locating pretty colored dolls to send to their new friends at Christmas time. Then the main building of the Southern school burned. "We'll have to do more than make scrapbooks now," said one of the girls with tears in her eyes. The entire girls' department was appealed to. Two plays were given and two hundred dollars was contributed toward the rebuilding of the school.

As commencement time approached, they discovered that a young colored girl, who had sung for them at their girls' conference, was to be the first girl of her race to graduate from their local high school. They learned that she wanted to go to college. After much discussion, they worked out this plan: They would raise three hundred dollars for the Sunday School Extension Society, ask them to employ this colored girl and have her conduct a Daily Vacation School in the church to which they had contributed the girls' dressing room. The girl would then be doing a real piece of service and be able to earn her way to college. With the aid of the junior and senior school boys' and girls' departments, they raised the money. On children's day came the fitting climax to the year's work. The colored girl told of the work of the Extension Society and, standing hand in hand with the daughter of the woman whom years ago her own mother had accompanied north as a maid, she received from her lips the commission of the school to go as their ambassador to the children of the city's slums. In these unforeseen by-projects, they did not cease to send to the little colored children in the South the "Heroines of Service" scrapbooks. They contained the lives of some noble colored women, of Florence Nightingale, Harriet Beecher Stowe, Alice Freeman Palmer, of Ruth, Esther and Miriam, and many others. "What did you learn from this project?" one of the girls was asked. "So many things," came the enthusiastic reply, "but especially this—if colored girls only had a chance, there would be just as many great colored women as there are great white women—if not more!"

DIFFICULTIES IN PROJECT TEACHING

Before closing this discussion of the project principle, it may be well to summarize a few of the objections or difficulties which are met as well as the advantages which are gained by its use.

One of the common dangers which is frequently pointed out is that a project may be viewed and be carried on as if it were merely a physical activity. This has been the difficulty in much of our social service. It has become often an outlet for something to do that is new and interesting. It must not be so. A project must be so directed that it has not only physical activity values, but, as we tried to point out in the foregoing illustrations, values affecting the head and the heart.

There is a real danger of haphazard, opportunist teaching, which leaves the pupil with no well defined or organized knowledge. Good project teachers will see to it that not only is each project brought to a proper conclusion in this respect, but that a well rounded experience is the heritage of every child. There are numerous instances where classes of their own accord have asked for systematic study of the Bible, of church history, of codes of living and even of theological systems as projects of which they felt the need after catching a glimpse of their value in the course of project experiences of other types.

Many leaders fall into the temptation of having their pupils engage in projects which are not on the Christian level. There are plenty of institutions engaged in *good* projects; the church should be in the vanguard of the community forces in the type of projects which it and its learning members are carrying on. Projects with the personal touch, emphasizing human values, projects of constructive justice and the highest social welfare, projects which cause the individual experiencer to have a deep personal consciousness of his responsibility, projects which are *reconstructing* society as well as remedying bad situations, projects requiring real Christian thinking and arousing true Christian emotions, these are highly desirable and the absence of these types is a valid criticism of the effectiveness of the project concept as a principle of Christian education.

The most common objection made is on the ground that our teachers are not trained to do this kind of teaching. Venturing the assertion that they can be and are being trained to do this higher type of teaching, it may be said in passing that its acceptance means that we must raise the quality of the teaching we have been doing in religious education, even as we are, without the slightest protest, insisting upon better and better trained teachers in our public and private schools. The history of all education shows that every new advance in method has demanded a corresponding elevation of the standard of teaching. The church should be the last institution to stand still, if it believes in the supremacy of the contribution which it has to offer the world.

ADVANTAGES OF THE NEW PROCEDURE

In conclusion, we may refer again to some of the advantages which have been implied throughout our discussion. Project teaching gives the leader the distinct advantage of working *with* the pupil rather than against him, as has too often been the case in educational procedure. The point of departure is the spontaneous interest of the child, and this to a greater degree than ever before in teaching procedure. The processes of everyday life become one with the materials of education, thus representing a saving of time, money and effort, as well as doing away with a situation which frequently makes education appear to the child a strange and aimless procedure. Then, too, the growing Christian becomes an effectual ally of the church, not only contributing to the actual work which must be done but enlarging and renewing its ideals and fellowship. True project teaching reconciles the unfortunate dualism between the personal and social emphasis in religion; for in one and the same experience of loving service, the child comes to find a personal consciousness of the Ideal Companionship and a breadth of sympathy with his fellow men. It likewise offers a common central core for activities of instruction, worship and service for which leaders are seeking a basis of correlation. Finally, in these days of standard, uniform, and externally imposed programs, it gives large freedom to the individual teacher and the local church. They thus have the opportunity, so frequently desired, of developing a program of religious education which is indigenous to local conditions and creeds and which is sufficiently flexible to respond readily to the changes which do come and must come as each church finds an ever larger meaning in the challenge to build the kingdom of God.

FOR FURTHER STUDY

ARCHER, JOHN C. *A New Approach in Missionary Education.* Missionary Education Movement.

BETTS, GEORGE H. and HAWTHORNE, MARION O. *Method in Teaching Religion.* Abingdon Press.

GREGG, ABEL J. *Group Leaders and Boy Character.* Association Press.

KILPATRICK, WILLIAM H. *et al.* "Difficulties and Dangers of the Project Method and How to Overcome Them—A Symposium," *Teachers College Record,* volume XXII, pages 283-321.

LOBINGIER, JOHN L. *Projects in World Friendship.* University of Chicago Press.

SHAVER, ERWIN L. *Church School Projects.* University of Chicago Press.

SHAVER, ERWIN L. *The Project Principle in Religious Education.* University of Chicago Press.

"Teaching Religion by Projects" (a symposium), *Religious Education,* volume XXI, pages 436-536.

TOWNER, MILTON C. *One Hundred Projects for the Church School.* Doran.

WATSON, GOODWIN B. and GLADYS H. *Case Studies for Teachers of Religion.* Association Press.

See also reference list at conclusion of the preceding chapter.

CHAPTER FIVE

THE CHANGING CURRICULUM

The new concept of method in teaching religion brings us face to face with the question of curriculum. Method and curriculum have always been related in a complementary fashion. It is but natural, therefore, that we should take up the problem of the nature of the curriculum of religious education to discover what is happening and what the outcome will be.

It shall be the purpose of this chapter to discuss the problem under the following heads:

1. A brief sketch of the important phases of the development of the curriculum of religious education in modern times.

2. An interpretation of the theory which underlies the present day tendencies in curriculum building, and an evaluation of materials in the light of this theory.

3. An attempt to define the nature and scope of the coming curriculum and to show the facts in the present situation which indicate progress in the new direction.

4. Some practical suggestions for the more effective use of the materials which are now available.

CURRICULUM EMPHASES IN THE PAST

If we go back in the history of education about two hundred years, we find that the dominant theory which determined the choice of curriculum materials was the theory of discipline. The mind was viewed as possessing certain "faculties" which needed training. A few subjects, selected because of their supposed disciplinary powers, were the means whereby the several processes of reasoning, imagination, memory and the like were prepared for use in all the activities of life, regardless of their kinship to the subject matter of the schoolroom. Another emphasis which began about a century ago was the tendency to view the curriculum as a body of knowledge which must be transmitted by a certain skillful process called the "five formal steps." Before long, under this view, the curriculum came to include all the facts which a present society inherits from the history of the past. About a generation ago there arose a new emphasis, the theory of recapitulation. According to this theory, the curriculum materials for each sharply defined stage of the child's development are to be found in the corresponding period of the age of the race. Education in general and the theory of the curriculum up to the present time have been dominated by these three emphases. The disciplinary theory has disappeared under the pressure of a new psychology which has no place for separate mental faculties. The doctrine of recapitulation, although the incentive of many of our present day graded programs in religious education, no longer has a following in educational circles. But the emphasis upon the accumulated knowledge of the race as the primary content of the curriculum is only now being questioned.

It is this emphasis upon knowledge of the past which has found expression in various types of lesson materials in the American Sunday School during the past century and a quarter. In the early days of the Sunday school, as transplanted to American soil and taken over by the church, we find the content of the curriculum centering in the Bible and the catechism. The lessons consisted in memorizing great quantities of Scripture in a rather random fashion. Following this period from about 1825-1865, there developed a number of lesson courses which attempted to cover the Bible in some sort of systematic fashion. Out of this "Babel" period, as it has been called, came the Uniform Lesson System. This is still with us, but is rapidly being displaced by the Graded Lessons which were introduced in the early years of the present century. It was the knowledge of child life and development which accompanied the recapitulation doctrine, although not necessarily bound up with it, which led to the principle of the selection and adaptation of materials for which graded lessons stand.

THE NEW CONCEPT OF THE CURRICULUM

In all these periods, however, the knowledge view of the curriculum has been foremost. But within recent years a number of forces have been at work. Education has become a science in its own name; it has had the help of other sciences, such as psychology, biology and sociology; it has been influenced by the concept of the progressive development of society expressed in the doctrine of evolution; it has felt the pressure of the practical demands of modern life. Because of these factors, new emphases are finding expression, such as the emphasis upon learning through activity, upon the social nature of the learning process and upon the principles of continuity and adjustment to ever-changing life situations. These points of view have brought about a new concept of the curriculum as experience which we shall now discuss.

One of the best statements of this somewhat revolutionary concept is found in the Report of Commission V on the Church and Education to the Universal Christian Conference on Life and Work.[1] The report says: "The curriculum of the church school should be experiential in character, and its program of organization inclusive. . . . The church school should be, not so much a place where children may learn something or other about religion, as a place where they may experience religion. It should be a fellowship of children associated in Christian living, under the leadership of the Church, and consequently growing in Christian experiences and acquiring Christian habits, attitudes, motives, ideals and beliefs.

"The curriculum of the church school should therefore be pupil-centered, rather than material-centered, as Sunday school lessons have too often been. Instead of starting with a given body of material, and asking the question at what ages we may most profitably

[1]Held at Stockholm, Sweden—August 19-30, 1925.

teach the different sections of this material, a truer
method of curriculum-making starts with the children.
It asks what are the opportunities, problems and
experiences that are normal at each stage of developing
childhood; and it undertakes so to order the situations
into which it brings children and the material which it
makes accessible to them, as to help them meet these
opportunities, solve these problems and have these
experiences.

"The church school, so conceived, is inclusive. It
cannot be confined merely to the Sunday hour, or to
the type of effort which the Sunday school has ordinarily represented. Its curriculum embodies more than
instruction; it includes the experience of worship, the
experiences of fellowship, of giving, of cooperation,
of service—indeed, the whole range of experiences that
enter normally into the development of Christian life
and character. And so the church school will include,
as an organic part of its program and organization, all
lesser clubs, societies and groups which the church
maintains for the Christian education of its children
and young people. The church school is another name
for the church itself, undertaking, with a consciously
educative purpose, to make its own life and experience
available to oncoming generations."

SOME DISTINCTIVE CHARACTERISTICS

An analysis of this new view of the curriculum as
based upon experience reveals a number of characteristics which we would like to point out.

1. The several distinct experiences or lessons which go to make up the total curriculum must be timely; that is, they must be so arranged that they are appropriate to the pupil's past experience and growth. This takes into account the principle of gradation which we have mentioned, but goes even further. There are many other factors than general periodic development which combine to make a pupil what he is at any given moment. His own individual characteristics and differences which distinguish him from "the average child," the previous training which he has received in his family, play and school life, and the entire scope of world environment in which he is living must be studied as well as "the psychological child," when one is selecting educative experiences.

2. These experiences must be naturally connected with the pupil's interests. The new point of view assures us that there are many doorways through which the child may be led into the world which he is to possess and that it is the teacher's opportunity to utilize those which his own native impulses open for him. We can be assured also that the child is not naturally evil in his inborn tendencies, but that there are many positive instinctive interests which may be seized upon as points of contact by the leader.

3. The experiences, as we have pointed out in our treatment of the project principle, must be life-like, real sections of the ongoing life of the whole church in whose midst the child is living. The nearer they are to the everyday work in which the church is engaged,

the more assured the teacher may be of the ideals and practices learned "carrying on" in other and later life situations.

4. To be truly educative these lesser units of the experience curriculum should be extremely vital and dynamic. It was this feature which our forefathers sought in the revival. The experience to the child must be a "red-letter" event, vivid, impressive, thought-provoking, emotion-arousing, one which he can long remember.

5. Not only must these lesson-experiences be dynamic in the sense we have defined, but also dynamic in effect; that is, they must be habit-forming, reaching the child's entire life organism. They must not be experiences solely of information and inspiration, but of doing something that is worthwhile on the Christian level. This means, also, that the new act must be repeated until it becomes veritably a part of muscle and bone and sinew.

6. The project undertaken is not to be viewed as complete, or its educative value as conserved, until the teacher and pupils together have interpreted it. This is, as it were, the process of gathering the fruit. Not forgetting that a lesson is not learned by the sole process of interpretation, any more than fruit is obtained by the final stage of ingathering, we may assure ourselves that it is important that as an integral part of the total experience a place be given to discovering and fixing its meaning.

7. Desirable experience material for the new cur-

riculum must place the individual learner in a social world. The truly personal experience of religion does not mean an isolated experience; rather it means that it is a deep, intensive and meaningful affair. There is nothing exclusive about it. We go so far as to say that the most intense personal experiences are those in which there are the most far-reaching social implications.

8. The Christian is not receiving a true education unless the experiences he is having are of the *re*-creative type. He must learn from each experience to seek for higher values; in every lesson there must be some unfulfillment, a yearning to go on discovering and building a better world than that in which he finds himself.

9. It must be said, also, that the elements in a curriculum of experience must be economically acquired. Some things the pupil must find out for himself; other things he must take second-hand from his older and more experienced friends, and will purposefully and gladly do so if the proper relationship has been established.

THREE GENERAL SOURCES OF MATERIALS

If we again analyze the experience which is to enter into the new curriculum of religious education, we find it gathered from three sources. In the first place, it consists of the present events and happenings of the world in which the child lives daily. They are teaching him. They are his course in character building. They teach some desirable lessons, some not so desirable. Present experience must therefore be controlled and redirected. For this reason we must look to other sources, one of which is the past experience of those who have lived before him. By carefully introducing him to this past experience, as far as it is appropriate to his present interests and needs, we may hope to modify the present stream of experience. But even this source of help is not finally satisfactory. There are some lessons the past cannot teach us; for example, how to enforce prohibition, how to bring about international and interracial peace, and other conditions of a better social order. Consequently, we look not to the past alone, but to the future. We set going an experiment, it may be on a small scale. It may be largely initiated and carried on by children and youth who have the conviction born of uncrushed idealism, that Jesus' hypothesis of brotherhood is actually workable. All these sources, then, past, present and future, are contributors to the curriculum of Christian education.

EXISTING COURSES EVALUATED

In the light of this rather brief exposition of a curriculum based upon experience, we shall proceed to evaluate some of the existing curriculum materials of the church school. In view of space limitations, we can give only general criticisms without going into detail regarding the several series now available. A critical examination reveals such weaknesses as the following:

1. The courses offered are based too exclusively upon past experience. They take relatively little account of the present events which are having so powerful an effect upon the life of the child. It has been but recently that one could introduce, and then only in the face of considerable opposition, the lives and works of modern Christian evangels. One would not entirely ignore the experience of the kings of Israel and Judah, but it would seem that some more equitable distribution of emphasis should be made. And how few church-school classes ever have, as a part of their real curriculum, experiences of an experimental, or looking-forward-into-the-future nature, which so readily engage the interest and energy of the child's God-given instincts.

2. For the reason that the experience is so predominantly past in content it has to be introduced in book form. Education is therefore a matter of intellectual approach. One's emotions can not be very much aroused over these events of long ago which one reads about in a book or quarterly. Nor can one see much connection between living in those days and living now; consequently, there is little tendency to action and service. Even now we are trying to put together, by a patchwork process of correlation, the three phases of religious education known as instruction, worship and service, which in reality should be discovered as inseparable phases of a single unitary

experience. It is an almost universal practice to use the words "religious instruction" as synonymous with religious education. Our courses are too exclusively instructional.

3. Another criticism of our present materials is that they fail to be sufficiently adaptable. Demand on the part of local constituencies and competition among various publishing houses are bringing about some changes, but much is left to be desired. Children's interests and needs are quite ignored in our endeavor to "get across" adult viewpoints. Instead of preparing the child for a far-off adult life, we should prepare him to meet the problems of his own daily life in the Christian spirit, with the assurance that Christian living on the morrow will naturally follow. Another frequent criticism as to the adaptability of materials is that made by the local church, to the effect that the courses are not suited to its particular needs. We are only beginning to recognize the truth that every church is a "peculiar" church and must have materials adaptable to its situation, history and type.

4. Most of our courses have too little practical reference. They deal too largely with principles, which are good enough as principles, but fail unless they are inductively discovered in the practical experiences of every day. One cannot learn a principle by memorizing a statement of it or discussing it. One learns it, as we have pointed out, by engaging in an activity in which it is inherent. As further proof of the abstract emphasis in our present courses, we have the scant

attention paid to such questions as temperance, missions, social service, peace and other problems which are at the focus of the Christian consciousness at the present time. When we do teach these subjects, they come in as appendages to the curriculum rather than as central and essential experiences in which the great Christian principles are discovered and applied.

5. Another difficulty with our present curricula is their inflexibility. Every time we have had a change in materials we have rejoiced and said "Now we have it!" only to realize in a few years that they were beginning to be out of date. The thought of continuous progress has not been taken into account by curriculum builders. Many a local church which would like to move forward in its educational program has been held back by a static curriculum.

6. From two different angles the present curriculum is too individualistic. We have said that it ignores many of the present day problems which require the social emphasis of the gospel for their solution. We are not minded to speak of one gospel for the individual and another for society, for the two are inseparable and complementary. But we have not had in our lesson materials sufficient of the social note. In quite another way, also, the individualistic note is sounded. The learning process in character formation has been assumed to be that of each scholar learning his lesson quite apart from his fellows. In the best public schools we have cooperative learning as we have previously explained. Certainly in the process of

growth in Christian character, "we are many members of one body." An attempt to recognize this principle of learning through organized group activity has been made by promoting organized classes, but the movement has been ineffectual because it is viewed as an appendage to the curriculum. It would seem that we must have greater recognition of the cooperative element in the organization of the project-experiences which go to make up the curriculum.

These adverse criticisms which we have been making should not close our eyes to the fact that progress has been made in recent years in improving the curriculum. We have had an increasing emphasis upon gradation and adaptation of materials to age groups. We are finding more of the practical emphasis and have noted more liberal views in the interpretation of religion. The physical appearance of the printed materials used has changed. In place of the cheap quarterlies we are having more respectable pamphlets and books devoid of advertisements. Much of this advance has had to come through the wasteful process of competition and has often resulted in confusing the local church school as to the merits of the wide variety of courses available. But it has afforded better types of curricula for the forward-looking school and in turn furnished the backward school with a goal toward which to strive.

THE CURRICULUM OF THE FUTURE

We shall now endeavor to give a general outline of some of the salient features of the coming curriculum of the church school. One of the first things to be said is that it will be a course of experiences in living, a series of projects such as we have described. Activity will be the dominant note as it is of the Christian life. These experiences will at once give knowledge, develop attitudes, and form habits. Vastly more than so many pages of a text will be included. There will be experiences of organizing groups to carry out Christian purposes; there will be activities of service, recreation, worship and study; such sub-projects as committee work, dramatic performances, observation trips, manual activities, games and parties, chart- and poster-making, discussion meetings, prayer services, and countless other activities will all be entered upon with definite Christian motives.

There will not be a single standardized curriculum in the sense in which we now use that term. The curriculum materials made available by outside agencies will be regarded in the nature of a reference library or source of materials to be utilized when and as needed by the local group. From these helps each year the local church will build its own working curriculum which, however, will be subject to change as conditions require it and probably differ from year to year. The most nearly fixed quantity in the curriculum will be a framework of desirable goals and objectives, more permanent in respect to the general and ultimate principles of living required of a Christian, but modifiable when the more immediate experiences required to teach those principles in a local situation at a given time are considered. Thus we will have the type experience as the public school has the type study. It may be that this year happenings in China offer the occasion to teach international and interracial friendliness; another year it may be the situation in Mexico; in any event, brotherliness is taught.

One of the practical problems we must face in the use of such a source library of curriculum materials is the question of making the experience of each local school and overhead agency available and accessible to every other school and agency. This means that one of the next steps is the codification of all existing and future materials. It seems quite likely that through the viewpoint we have described, the way will be opened for the correlation of many of our conflicting agencies. Instead of promoting separate and competing programs, each will turn over its program materials and methods to be used, in whole or in part as seems best, by local religious education agencies.

In the coming curriculum there will be a shift in emphasis from the materials as such to the part played by the teacher or leader. It has been well said that the curriculum is ninety per cent teacher. It is a consolation for the worthy teacher that he or she is far more important than the textbook. Many a teacher has made Christian men and women of his pupils, who knew little scholastically, but who knew how to provide the right kind of experiences for a group of boys or girls and lived as a worthy example of the Christ in their midst. The curriculum, therefore, will take the form, not of so many facts to be told to pupils or about which they are to study and be questioned, but rather of a guide to method. The kind of experiences that are desirable will be suggested, the method of initiating them set forth, together with directions as to how the experiences may be carried forward and how lessons may be obtained from them, and then suggestions will be given as to sources of material for both leader and pupils. From the standpoint of the project principle as we have discussed it, these guides to method may be thought of as project plans, offered merely as suggestions to local leaders.

Progress Being Made

Now that we have set the goal for the curriculum that is to be, let us note what progress is being made to reach it. In the first place, practically all of our existing courses are undergoing revision or reconstruction. Four years ago Group Graded Lessons were substituted for the Uniform Lessons in the Primary and Junior departments. In 1927 similar Group Graded Lessons were issued for the Intermediate and Senior departments, although for these departments the Uniform Lessons will still be made available. Most of us thought that when we had introduced the Closely Graded Lessons the millenium had arrived in the matter of curriculum materials. But during the past few years, a number of the denominations have radically revised these lessons. The Northern and Southern Methodists and the Congregationalists, as a syndicate, are now practically reconstructing their present Graded Lessons with new outlines and topics and in some cases providing for correlated week-day materials. With this move we may say that the *International* Graded Lessons actually cease to exist and in their place we have a number of denominational graded series.

The advent of the week-day school, which we are to discuss later, has resulted in a number of new courses. Most prominent among these is the Abingdon Series published by the Methodist Book Concern. For some of the grades two or more courses are available. The series is quite widely used in the closely federated type of week-day schools and also in the schools of other denominations. An interesting feature from the standpoint of curriculum building is the fact that some time after these courses began to appear as a series of texts or bodies of story and information material, a series of teacher's manuals was inaugurated. This illustrates what we have said about the teacher being the key factor in the educational process. The Congregational Publishing Society has also begun a series of courses based upon the activity principle, not as many in number as the Methodist series, but more truly representative of the advanced educational approach we have been describing. The Presbyterian and Baptist denominations have inaugurated a curriculum for a three-session-a-week church school, Sunday morning, Sunday evening, and midweek. The courses are largely content centered, but do show a bold attempt to build a correlated program independent of extra-church agencies. In experimental courses for vacation schools, the Reformed Church has produced Primary and Junior Conduct Programs which are quite in advance of the usual curriculum material for such schools.

Without the denominations we have an advance step taken by the University of Chicago Press in developing a new series of courses of a problem and project type and in planning to revise the Bible-centered courses of the Constructive Studies Series. The Missionary Education Movement has published several series of graded texts for mission study and also several single courses of the problem and project type. The discussion courses of the Association Press are finding a large place in classes of young people and adults. Then, too, we have a number of week-day schools where teachers have developed their own courses, notably at Gary, Indiana, Melrose, Massachusetts and Dayton, Ohio.

Nor is this all. In addition to the changes we have described as taking place, greater changes are promised. At the request of the International Lesson Committee the Department of Research and Service of the International Council of Religious Education has begun the development of experimental units of a proposed new International Curriculum, based upon the theory we have outlined. Twenty-seven prominent religious educators, representing fourteen denominations, persons who had had both thorough training and much experience in curriculum construction, assembled in Chicago for a three weeks' session of conference and work in March of last year. The result was a large "Blue Book" of sample units, necessarily hastily outlined and incomplete in form, but quite indicative of modern trends in religious education. The Department of Research and Service is at work upon the completion of the most promising of these units and will supervise experimentation with them in a number of centers.

Then again we must mention the research work being done by the Institute of Social and Religious Research at Teachers College, Columbia, under the title of the Character Education Inquiry, which promises to give us some very scientific evidence as to the processes by which the characters of growing children are actually formed and which may result in an entire re-study of curriculum theory. All in all, it looks as though one might reasonably expect an array of new curriculum materials for some time to come!

USING PRESENT MATERIALS MORE EFFECTIVELY

Since most leaders, however, must use the materials that are now available, we will endeavor to indicate a few of the ways by which such materials can be enriched to provide more educative experiences of the type we have described.

1. The teacher using material of any character should become thoroughly acquainted with the interests, needs and problems of the members of his class. He will then be able to teach pupils rather than lessons.

2. He should use the lesson material offered in the text or quarterly as a source of help from which he may select those portions most timely and adaptable to his pupils' needs. It is not necessary that he use all the material just as given.

3. He should proceed to enrich this text material with other experiences from reference books and from his own personal life. He should utilize maps, charts, pictures and other objective aids. Above all, he should plan definitely to have the pupils bring into the class for discussion their own experiences on the playground, in the home and school, and from the wider community and world life.

4. All these sources of help should then be analyzed and interpreted in a democratic fashion. In this phase of the lesson great emphasis should be placed upon the practical application of the principles discovered in the source material. One may be safe in saying that at least one-half of the time available should be spent in this manner.

5. It is better to spend more than one session on a lesson in which vital interest has been developed than to hurry on to the next material. Not the number of experiences, but impressive, "red-letter" experiences, should be the motto of the teacher.

6. But no Christian teacher should limit his teach-

ing to the class hour. The best teachers of all ages have never done so. A church-school teacher should regard the extra-class lessons as important as those in the class. Therefore, he should provide for his pupils' learning the Christ way in activities of play, of worship and of service. He should find a place for them to share democratically in the ongoing life and work of the church. "The church considered as educator," says Coe, "is primarily a fellowship of older and younger persons." No amount of textbook teaching can be a substitute for this richer program of experiences, which any devoted teacher can carry on with his class.

FOR FURTHER STUDY

BOWER, WILLIAM C. *The Curriculum of Religious Education.* Scribner.

CASE, ADELAIDE T. *Liberal Christianity and Religious Education.* Chapter VI. Macmillan.

COE, GEORGE A. *A Social Theory of Religious Education.* Chapter IX. Scribner

COE, GEORGE A. "Opposing Theories of the Curriculum," *Religious Education,* volume XVII, pages 143-150.

COPE, HENRY F. *Organizing the Church School.* Pages 112-115 and chapter XXI. Doran.

LANKARD, FRANK G. *A History of the American Sunday School Curriculum.* Abingdon Press.

MACLEAN, ANGUS H. "Religious Curricula and Science," *Religious Education,* volume XXIII, pages 141-148.

"Principles and Procedure in Curriculum Construction" (a symposium), *Religious Education,* volume XXI, pages 567-617.

SHAVER, ERWIN L. *The Project Principle in Religious Education.* Chapter VIII. University of Chicago Press.

SHAVER, ERWIN L. *A Project Curriculum for Young People.* University of Chicago Press.

Examine also a number of the more recent courses offered for use in the church school.

CHAPTER SIX

WHAT OF THE BIBLE?

One question which is sure to be asked, in view of all that has been said about the new type of curriculum in the preceding chapter, is: "But where does the Bible come in?" It is but natural and right that this problem should be faced and within the limits of the few pages set aside to treat of it we shall face it squarely.

It needs no lengthy argument to show that there is a good deal of discussion with regard to the use of the Bible in religious education as we know it today. Various "schools" of educationists in this field are taking varied and often opposing viewpoints. One notes these differences when it comes to shaping up the content and method of new types of curricula, wherever workers get together for this purpose. The sport of dragging dusty characters out of the Old Testament as well as out of other records of past achievement to satisfy one's hunting instincts is an especial favorite with magazine writers and the popular type of iconoclast, both secular and ecclesiastical. Other groups of folk, in great alarm, are calling for the teaching of the Bible in the public schools on the grounds that the present and rising generations have no knowledge of its contents and that the only way to rid the world of crime waves is to digest the contents of the fine old Book. "To teach or not to teach the Bible"—this is the question of the day.

It is bootless to take up the problem without first making some analysis of the factors which have given rise to the present situation. We desire first, therefore, to call attention to some of these causal or explanatory antecedents in the hope that an examination of them will help us to answer the question of our chapter.

RESULTS OF BIBLICAL CRITICISM

The rapid spread of the scientific viewpoint and the growth of such sciences as geology, physics, biology, psychology, and many others, began more than a generation ago to undermine faith in the Bible. The first instinctive reaction of defense has crystallized the minds of many into blind acceptance of unscientific views of the religious life. Only gradually have a small minority been able to find a place for the Bible as a modern guidebook in lofty living in spite of the fact that it was written in a pre-scientific age. The great mass of folk, however, have held a hazy and unstable view of it all, which has resulted in a religion which they fell back upon only in life's crises and one which they hesitated to teach to their children, who were being grounded in the scientific viewpoint at every turn.

The first results of criticism were necessarily felt to be destructive. Perhaps, when we enter a period of civilization where we expect and plan for progress and distinguish between truth and its "effluence," as Lowell puts it, we shall not view new ideas as destructive. The tendency was to say: "If I can't believe *all* the Bible, I won't believe *any* of it." This atmosphere of tearing down has been with us even until now. It is to be hoped that we can quickly pass on to a more constructive atmosphere and preach the marvelous and almost revolutionary implications of the new approach for the Kingdom of God, instead of resting content with having acquired the intellectual smugness which marks the illiberal liberal.

The present picture is that of confusion. We see two views of truth arrayed one against the other without an understanding of the fact that, when rightly interpreted, both are sound. But for most people, including many religious educators, the only solution has been to give way a step at a time to scientific advances. One notes, with mingled feelings of satisfaction and expectant waiting, the shifts in viewpoint with regard to the reinterpretation and choice of certain Old Testament materials for little children by writers and preachers. Until we come to certain well defined principles which are more or less permanent, we shall have confusion of thinking and suspicion of the Bible as a source book for the development of twentieth century Christian character.

There is a steady reaction against what has almost amounted to Bible worship among Protestants. This reaction is one which many would welcome, for bibliolatry is as dangerous as blind devotion to the dictates of an infallible Church. But one result of this reaction has been to substitute present-day ethical judgments and standards as our highest goals instead of searching, amid what may be of lesser value, for the priceless pearls which will purchase humanity's salvation.

NEW EDUCATIONAL VIEWPOINTS

Modern educational theory tells us that we are not to teach subjects, but rather to teach children and youth. Doubtless this is sound, even though we shall probably find still newer ways of stating educational aims which include the child-centered goal. Our previous chapters have given sufficient illustration of this shift of attention on the part of the teacher. With this change of focus in mind one can easily understand why one hesitates to speak of teaching the Bible. It does not necessarily mean less respect for the Bible sources, but a new approach in their use. It must be said, however, that one result has been a setting aside of large portions of the Bible as unsuitable for children of certain ages and some portions of it as unsuited to any age.

The doctrine of recapitulation as applied to psychological development and to the choice of curriculum materials has no longer any followers among religious educators of standing. Space forbids a discussion of this fact except to say that its application meant that the various types of literature for Christian education purposes should be taken from the periods of the Christian development of the race; that is, little children should study the early creation stories first, then follow as Juniors with the heroes of Israel as they passed through the "stage" of hero worship, then move on through the Bible and arrive somewhat later at the New Testament period. In its bald literalness the theory never influenced our religious education literature as it did the public school curricula and the programs of the early extra-church character-building agencies. But it obtained enough of a hold to give justification for using the host of Old Testament stories which are just now giving curriculum writers and teachers so much trouble. What is happening is a growing disinclination to use much of the Old Testament for small children.

Close upon this has come the realization that the Bible was not written for children. If we begin with the child and ask what will be most helpful in the way of story materials to help him meet his present problems, and set up certain standards of selection such as ethical value, adaptation to his experience, style of writing, and similarity of problem, we find that large sections of what we have been in the habit of using are decidedly inappropriate, provided we can for the moment of judgment free ourselves from the notion, "we must teach it because it's in the Bible."

A host of general education influences have led us to lay less emphasis upon the use of the Bible. The gradation of materials, the emphasis upon the explanation and discussion of principles and precepts rather than their memorization, the use of printed texts and source materials as well as all sorts of illustrative enrichment, the increasing introduction of interesting teaching methods and devices—all these and other procedures have tended to push the actual handling and use of the Bible into the background.

GROWTH OF ETHICAL DISCRIMINATION

A considerable number of Christian teachers are using what are sometimes called ethical and social problems courses. They are desirous of finding the meaning of Bible principles for the life of today and take this method. Somehow there has been that at work in the past use of the Bible which has acted as a leaven to demand a criticism of present practices in the light of Biblical principles. Some of these courses maintain a high Christian standard of ethics even though they use relatively less of Biblical source material than did former types of lessons. Others are quite devoid, not only of Biblical source material, but of any reference to there being a distinctively Christian solution of the problem at hand.

In quite another way the growth of ethical discrimination on the Christian level has resulted in a decreasing use of the Bible. There has developed out of the materialistic emphasis in our civilization a pragmatic type of thinking which shies at the idealism of Jesus as quite ethereal and impracticable of application to the problems of life today. Some of these call themselves Christian and demand, for obvious reasons, "plain Bible lessons" for children; some, as they discover that more and more religious education leaders lean toward sharp insistence upon high ideals, cease to be interested in the Bible or in the church.

In proportion as the lofty principles of Jesus have become manifest in modern Bible study so has the unworthiness of certain pre-Christian and sub-Christian codes of living found in the Bible become more apparent. It is the presence of these very low moral standards, aided by educational practices of teaching the Bible rather than children and of using a literal, proof-text method, which has enabled the opponents of Christian reform to block progress and cause confusion among well intentioned Christians. As we cease to employ these materials both because of their low ideals and because of the predominantly negative approach to character education which their use involves, it does seem that considerable portions of the Bible are becoming of less and less value as materials of Christian education.

Another factor under the heading we are here discussing is the discovery that other literatures written since the close of the Biblical canon have inspirational and instructional values. Recent years have seen an abundance of such materials used. Nor are those who are religious educators in the restricted sense the only users of such materials. The preaching ministry has made as large a use of them, if not more. Here again, although the religious educator would urge their use on several grounds, the fact that they do show the continuous revelation of the Christian God is sufficient justification for many to employ them.

Similarly, with the extension of the true missionary spirit and the growth of the world into a neighborhood of peoples all seeking after God, there has come the realization that He has not left himself without witness among any people and that the literatures of many cultures are filled with His spirit. Hence it is increasingly apparent that the Christian thing to do is to welcome every utterance, by whatsoever mouthpiece God has chosen to speak. The Bible by this fact ceases to be the only word of God.

THE BIBLE IN CURRICULUM CHANGES

As we briefly note the transitions which have occurred in the last generation in the curriculum materials used in our church-schools, we see again the influence of many of the foregoing factors. But we also see other factors at work to affect the amount and character of the Biblical materials used. The Uniform Lessons, still used in perhaps half of our Sunday schools, found it best to print sections of the Bible and gradually we ceased to use the book itself. The Closely Graded Lessons do not print the scripture selections, but refer to them with the hope that the Bible will be used as a reference book. The hope, however, remains largely a hope, for the habits of two generations are not easily broken. It should be said in passing that careful investigation has shown that the Graded Lessons have made use of a much larger total of Biblical materials than their Uniform predecessors and also have included a wider selection and more choice portions. The special types of courses now becoming popular for the most part either print little of the Bible or print small excerpts bearing upon the point under discussion. It is hard to predict, but it would appear that the type of curriculum toward which we are just now drifting may unfortunately confine its use of the Bible to just such a fragmentary approach.

SOURCE VALUES OF THE BIBLE

We are now ready to make certain positive statements as to the place of the Bible in our modern program of religious education. In the light of the factors which we have just been considering and in view of the discussions of foregoing chapters of this book, we venture the following:

1. The Bible is to be used as a partial source of the new curriculum of religious education. There are a number of reasons for this. If religious education is to seek for the child and youth a vital experience of God, it is apparent that something more than Bible memorization or study must be brought to bear to produce that experience. At the best, study is only one aspect of a Christian experience; there must be in addition an environing of his situation so that his emotions are aroused and he feels the presence of God and of all the children of God; and further, the experi-

ence must provide for that taking place which actually habituates him in his daily life to make responses which are Christian. All these are sources of his training materials. Bible study is but one.

The value of the Bible is further limited in that it is merely a record of past experience. Past experience gives guidance; but it is living, present experience which makes habits and affects character. Even the guidance of past experience is limited, for there are countless problems of Christian living facing us today for which neither the present nor the past experience has any solution, except the dreams of the prophets and the faith of Jesus. There is a real sense in which we might say that the child must be introduced to an experience which is future, an experiment in finding a new way of life which no one has discovered, if his Christian education is to be complete.

Beyond this, there are further limitations. The Bible represents the past experience of a limited period of time and is confined to that of one people. Is it presumptuous to say in the face of the vast array of historical and scientific facts which reveal the presence of the Living God long before the Bible was even in story form and long after its canon was closed, that its pages are after all but a partial revelation of his love for men? And is it presumptuous to say, in the face of the fine utterances that are coming from the literatures and the spoken words of many witnesses in other parts of the earth as our missions program becomes one of world friendship and appreciation, that we may not learn something from each people and use whatever Christlike word or deed we find to teach our children His way? We think not.

2. The Bible is to be used as the qualitative source of the new curriculum of religious education. What we have just said would seem to limit the Bible to a rather narrow field in consideration of the total materials to be employed. From the standpoint of quantity this may be true. But from the standpoint of quality we believe we are not Pharisaical if we hold that the loftiest ideals and the loftiest examples are to be found in its pages. It does contain many typical experiences which may be brought to bear from the past to redirect the present life situations of the child. There is a place even for its negative approaches and its records of failure to achieve. But these are of small moment beside its supreme value of giving us the standard by which the value of all other materials within and without its pages are to be measured. The gladly given testimony of peoples of other religious faiths is more and more to the effect that the standards and life of Jesus are those they are willing to accept, provided we can strip our religion of its non-essential trappings and practice what he preached by word and deed. If the Bible is shrinking as a quantitative source of materials for Christian education, it is on the other hand coming into its own as a qualitative source.

3. The Bible thus becomes, by this fact and because of the findings of modern scholarship and experience, a source for the principles of Christian living rather

than a source of literal examples. It is hard to overcome the habit of asking ourselves, "What would Jesus do?" and of seeking the answer in what he did in a quite dissimilar situation. Our answer is best found in the principles of his life, which may or may not be illustrated in the situation with most literally similar characteristics. That is why he is so hard to understand and so hard to follow, and so much The Teacher of the Ages. Our Bible, used in this way for its principles, should not appear to be of lesser value, but of far greater and more lasting worth.

4. The Bible, because of the limitations we have placed upon it and because of the new values we have sought to emphasize, is a source of the "symbols" and "codes" of the Christian experience we would like our children to have. The principles, the words it contains, are, like the Word it reveals, to be made flesh and dwell among us for the child to behold and react to so that they may become the "drives" for his own thought and feeling and conduct. Thus our task is to provide flesh for what are otherwise but dry bones. As far as practicable and economical, we are to lead our pupils into and through the present and first hand experiences which will effect the results implied by the great life-purpose symbols found in the Bible. We are not to mistake the symbol for the experience and try by short-cut process to feed the child upon the dry husk, but provide for him the kernel of life which it holds. With this in mind, let us thank God for the great symbols to be found in the Bible.

5. The Bible, from all that we have said above, may be characterized as the dynamic source of religious education for all times. It is, as men have found from experience, not a closed book, but an ever-enlarging revelation of God, tuned to each new generation and its many problems. Without the specific guidance of a literal lesson on slavery men saw its inconsistency with the spirit of Christ and solved the problem; likewise with strong drink, in the face of literal examples even to the contrary; so it will be with every new problem. The Bible is self-revealing, growing, pregnant with new truth to him who searches with loving heart, with open mind and determination of purpose.

THE MODERN USE OF THE BIBLE

In concluding this chapter, let us summarize what seem to be the ways in which we are to use the Bible as curriculum material for the new program of religious education. We may begin by saying that we are bound as truth seekers and as Christians to approach it in the scientific spirit, but remembering that the spirit of the real scientist is one of appreciation and of earnest desire to be helped and to help others. No truth-compromising spirit will bring messages from its pages, nor will a captious and destructive attitude devoid of the spirit of sympathetic love for all mankind.

We are to use the Bible as a source book containing the answers to the problems of life—problems relatively individual (if there be such) and problems which affect the wider circle of God's children. The book is not to be worshipped for its own sake and as an end. But we are to go to it as a means to an end, with a fervent desire to help somewhere and right now. We are to set children and youth and older folk, too, at work upon the building of the Kingdom of God and then show them how the Good Book contains the foundation stones. This means that a working, a serving, a loving church can teach its youth and the strangers within its gates only to the extent that it is itself a living and dynamic example of the Bible symbols it holds up.

In using the Bible as religious education source materials in this spirit, there will be two approaches. One will be the so-called "fragmentary" approach in which the students go to the Great Source Book and to other places and persons to find the ways to meet the problems of Kingdom building. Perhaps we may say that this will be the first approach. As the Bible is thus gradually revealed as the dynamic source of answers to life's deepest needs, the student will gladly undertake a systematic study of whole portions of it and of its origin. He will do this both for the sake of understanding its various principles which are less clear when studied in isolation and for the sake of being forehanded in meeting new situations still beyond his horizon. The curriculum will therefore include, among other types of units, those which use sections of the Bible as source materials to solve the pressing problems of individual and social life and those which study the Bible in systematic and organized wholes.[1]

When we do approach the Bible as the Great Answer Book of life, we are more likely, as we should be, to see in its pages living personalities who wrestled with problems like in temper if not in detail to those which we face. It is only as the Bible becomes a living book and the personalities it depicts become flesh and blood like ourselves that we can make proper use of it as a source book in modern religious education.

One great change in the manner of the use of the Bible which may seem to reverse our former policies is involved in the suggestion that we should introduce it to children gradually. Do we not now urge the child to memorize as much as he can of its abstract principles because we are afraid he may later lose his love for the church-school? Would it not be better to wait for systematic study of large portions of it until it comes more natural, believing that, if the little child found the Christian way of life a delight and its fellowship the kind he preferred above all else, he would more and more enter upon the appropriation of its deeper and more abstract truths?

First, we should, it seems to the writer, be content with a few simple principles with simple illustrations taken from life near at hand in time and place, with the least possible emphasis upon the failures to attain, taking it for granted that the Christian life is a chal-

[1] See the author's *A Project Curriculum for Young People,* pages 14-23; 31-35.

lenging and enjoyable thing. Then as the years pass, we would move on to more complex problems, with illustrations more removed in place and time. This means that those portions of Bible experience which depend upon the concept of the passage of time would be used only when the child had come to understand something of history, and those passages which have to do with the unexplained facts (miracles) only after some concept of a God whose world is one of cause and effect had been obtained. Such a principle of gradation must replace the recapitulation theory of gradation we are now discarding.

One of the greatest shifts of viewpoint which is yet to come to religious education in the use of the Bible and other materials is that of taking the positive rather than the negative approach to the building of Christian character. Our courses are almost entirely based upon the assumption that the child has committed or is about to commit some sin. We turn his attention constantly to his defects. We therefore make up lists of virtues and drill upon them. Might we not suggest that, if we were to ask children to assist us as junior partners in the great positive enterprises of building the Kingdom of God, the challenge and the real legitimate thrill of it all would cause them to develop true Christian character as a by-product, an almost unconscious accompaniment of fellowshiping with Christian people in the Christian enterprise? Then, as negative ways of acting arose, they could be dealt with as the obstacles to sharing in this achievement with others and could be changed much more easily because they would be seen as destroyers of fellowship. And might we not have faith, as Jesus did, that as one seeks to lose his life in the great adventure of serving humanity, he will find it! Our curriculum materials from the Bible, then, must be such that they lend themselves to this ongoing, positive approach which should occupy by far the larger portion of our total program of training.

Finally, in using the Bible sources, we should keep our own eyes and those of our pupils upon its highest ideals. There are plenty of agencies ready and eager to teach the things which are to be believed; there are few which are willing to pioneer on the frontiers of higher living. The Bible is preeminently a "Book of Holy Discontent" and in its pages we may find ideals which no other books have, ideals so far above our present social codes that it will require, as it always has, a divine fearlessness to urge men to follow after them. The best program of religious education for today, in its use of the rich sources from the Book of the Ages, must avail itself of these highest ideals which it alone contains.

FOR FURTHER STUDY

EISELEN, FREDERICK C. *A Christian View of the Old Testament.* Abingdon Press.

ELLIOTT, HARRISON S. *The Bearing of Psychology upon Religion.* Association Press.

FOSDICK, HARRY E. *The Modern Use of the Bible.* Macmillan.

GOODSPEED, EDGAR J. *The Story of the New Testament.* University of Chicago Press.

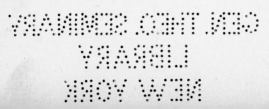

HUNTING, HAROLD B. *The Story of Our Bible.* Scribner.

KNAPP, FORREST L. "Educating for World Friendship," *The International Journal of Religious Education,* volume IV, number 6, pages 26-27.

MYERS, CHARLES H. "Jimmie Goes to Sunday School," *Scribner,* February, 1927.

"Religion and Science" (a symposium), *Religious Education,* volume XXIII, pages 89-163.

SHELDON, FRANK M. *The Bible in Our Modern World.* Pilgrim Press.

STREIBERT, MURIEL. *Youth and the Bible.* Macmillan.

WIEMAN, HENRY N. *The Wrestle of Religion with Truth.* Macmillan.

Chapter Seven

A CHURCH SCHOOL FOR THE WEEK DAY

The movement for week-day religious education is both old and new. It is old in the sense that we have always had some form of religious training on the week-day. In the early church there were the catechetical classes; in colonial days the Bible was the central textbook of the secular school; today we have a multitude of societies and clubs with character building objectives, which hold meetings on the week-day. But the agency we are to discuss is unique, not only from the standpoint of its organization, but to some extent also in content and method of teaching. Because of its origin, the week-day church school is often referred to as religious education "in cooperation with the public schools," although perhaps twenty-five per cent of the classes are not held on public school time. But whether using public school time or not, this new type of religious education is based on the thesis that religion is a fundamental factor in the total education of every child. A more precise understanding of its nature will be gained as we proceed.

GROWTH OF WEEK-DAY SCHOOLS

Although the historical development of the movement is interesting, we can dwell upon it only in passing. The first week-day schools of the type we have defined began in Gary, Indiana, in the fall of 1914. The Protestant pastors of Gary had protested to Superintendent Wirt that the lengthened school day so crowded the time and used the energy of the children that other agencies did not have a fair opportunity in their work with them. Dr. Wirt therefore suggested that the churches avail themselves of the free time periods, which are one of the many new features of the public school system in that city, to carry on religious education. At first the churches conducted their individual classes; then in 1918 a Board of Religious Education, representing most of the Protestant churches, was organized to conduct a system of schools which holds classes at the present time in nine centers. Van Wert, Ohio, in 1918 and Batavia, Illinois, in 1919 initiated week-day schools, the former of the inter-church type as now running in Gary and the latter of the earlier Gary type. In 1922 the writer made the first general survey of the growing movement and secured reports from 324 schools. At that time it was estimated that there were probably six hundred schools with a total enrollment of fifty thousand pupils. At the present time a conservative estimate would place the total at twenty-five hundred schools representing twelve or fifteen hundred communities and enrolling two hundred and fifty thousand pupils.

Causes of the Week-Day Movement

One might discover a number of causes contributory

to the development of this movement. There are two, however, which are significant and fundamental. The first of these is the demand for *more* religious education. The results we have been attempting to secure in the way of character development for childhood and youth cannot be obtained through the inefficient program of the old-fashioned Sunday school. Of the varied efforts to supplement it, the week-day movement is one of the most energetic. It is the spontaneous reaction of Protestantism to the many evils of the day and the apparent indifference to adequate religious standards. The second reason for the growth of week-day schools is found in the fact of their connection with the public school, namely the demand for an *educational* approach in propagating religion. The increasing appreciation of education as a means of producing desired results in thought and conduct in other phases of life is here applied to religion. The week-day school typifies Protestantism resuming its teaching function with serious purpose.

PRESENT STATUS DESCRIBED

One of the facts to be understood at the outset of a discussion of the week-day movement is the several types of schools. A school organized by a local church without reference to what other churches may be doing is called an *individual* or *denominational* school. When a number of churches organize and administer their own schools separately, but work together in such matters as in the approach to the public school board

for securing time or credit, in common publicity and
promotion, in coordinating time schedules, and in
other common interests, the schools established are
known as *denominational-cooperating* or *loosely federated* schools.   A third type, more commonly but
inaccurately called *community* schools, is like that at
Gary where the schools are carried on without regard
to denominational lines.   The government of the
schools is in the hands of a board directly representative of the churches.   A common curriculum is used
and the teaching, supervision and all other matters are
controlled by the inter-denominational board.   These
schools may be called *city systems* or *closely federated*
schools.   In the matter of government, the schools
now operating at Melrose, Massachusetts, are quite
different from any of the above types.   They are like
the closely federated schools just mentioned, but are
governed by a board which is representative of the
interested Protestant constituency, although not of
the churches directly.

At this point we shall also give a few facts regarding the organization and administration of the schools.
The budget is raised in various ways including public
subscription, pro-rata assessment among the cooperating churches, and occasionally by gifts from overhead
denominational agencies.   This money is expended for
workers' salaries, textbooks, office supplies and other
materials.   The classes meet in churches, parish
houses, and in specially erected buildings in a few
instances.   A relatively small number are held in the

public school building. The equipment is usually better than that of the Sunday school, but not of the quality of the public school. Although a few schools maintain classes for the entire range of grades, kindergarten, grammar school and high school, most of them are confined to the children of grammar school age with work in the fourth, fifth and sixth grades being most frequent. Two public school grades are usually combined to make one class in the school of religion. In releasing pupils from the public school, a written permit from the parent is required and the classes are so arranged that pupils are excused from a study period, from a play or auditorium period, or from recitation in an elective or supplemental subject. Class periods vary in length, the usual time being an hour once a week, although there seems to be a tendency to increase this to two hours a week. Surveys have shown that less than half of the teachers are paid, but there is a steady drift toward the salaried teacher. The previous training of half the teachers has fitted them for work of this type; the other half have had rather meager professional equipment.

The curriculum materials used are of wide variety. Whereas, at first, the Bible and Sunday school lessons were utilized, an increasing number of specially prepared courses have been developed both by denominational and private publishing houses. Some of these are for week-day schools only; others have correlated the Sunday and week-day program. In most schools the "knowledge" view of the curriculum predominates.

The course is viewed as so many ideas and facts which are to be made the possession of the pupil. Experiences of worship and service at first found little or no place in the program, although now there is a tendency to include these and other activities as well. An increasing number of schools and teachers are developing their own curricula.

One also finds in week-day schools great divergence in teaching methods. This is accounted for by the fact that many schools take their standards from the Sunday schools of their community, while others are avowedly seeking to do a superior grade of work. We find catechetical and drill methods in many schools. A few use preaching and lecture methods. A very large number are following text study. Some few schools have teachers who are basing their teaching upon the problems which they discover in the daily conduct of their pupils. By discussion and various types of project activities in which the pupils participate, they are being led to form new purposes and new habits. This latter approach is slowly but surely being recognized as the desirable method of dealing with the problems of children in week-day classes.

In discussing the present status of the week-day movement, a word should also be said regarding the relation of the week-day school to other agencies working with the child. Thus far we have only the beginnings of any cooperation in the case of the home. There is not the close relationship between the week-day school and the church which exists in the case of the Sunday school. This is due to the fact that one fourth of the week-day pupils are not in attendance upon a Sunday school, to a type of organization in many schools which has made correlation of program impossible, to the employment of professionally trained teachers and to differences in educational standards. The relations with the public school teachers and officers are for the most part unofficial. They are confined to the adjustment of time schedules and in a few cases to mutual correlation of the materials of instruction where teachers are awake to such possibilities.

RELATION TO PUBLIC SCHOOL

Following this brief survey of the week-day movement, let us consider some of the problems which must be solved if it is to make a worthwhile contribution to the total program of religious education. One of the most outstanding and pressing of these problems is that of the official and legal relation of the new institution to the public school. One of the leaders in the movement rightly prophesied several years ago that the movement would pass through three stages: "First, rapid and intensive propaganda concerning the idea, resulting in a widespread, mushroom growth; second, a period of legal fighting for existence; third, the recognition that the life of the movement must depend upon a higher set of standards, which, if once established in the week-day, would work their way back into the Sunday and in this way raise the old level of religious education."

While these stages overlap, we may safely say that we are now in the second stage. The legal disputes which have arisen bring up the old question of the relation of church and state. The writer believes that there are serious dangers in the promotion of week-day schools as it has been carried on in many quarters. To some the movement actually means that the public school is to teach religion; to a very large number there is much that is appealing and advantageous in the idea that the child be taught religion while he is, as it were, under the beneficent shadow of public school discipline and habits of study. The church is to lean upon this crutch fashioned for it by the state; it is asking the state school, with the ultimate authority of the law, to assist it in teaching religion, the fundamental basis of which is not law but the freely. given authority of the individual conscience.

It is those who take this position who have brought about many of the legal disputes. They have not observed the warnings which have been given. In some communities the churches have attempted to force the hand of the public school authorities with utter disregard of the consequences. Their only thought has been to secure a majority vote or the decision of an official. Little regard has been given to the careful education of public opinion and the correlative responsibility of guaranteeing, if time is granted, that the quality of work done shall be on a par with that of the public school.

In many communities in the early years of the

movement, the right of the local school authorities to excuse pupils for purposes of religious training was taken for granted as a custom long respected. When, however, the week-day school idea spread, it appeared to be something new, as it indeed was, as far as its extent was concerned. The writer has always maintained, however, that much more would be gained by assuming the existence of this old custom and making good use of time thus given than by seeking to secure a decision or pass a state enabling act.

What, then, is the relation that should exist between the church and state school in this new movement? It would seem that there are two principles which should be observed. One is the complete and unequivocal separation of church and state. The other is the right of each institution to a fair share of the time of the child and the right of each to educate the child acording to its particular objective. This sharing of educational responsibility and of deciding upon a mutually satisfactory division of the time should be done in the heartiest spirit of cooperation and understanding. On the one hand, we must bear in mind the multitude of calls which come to the public school officials to use the school as a propaganda agency for movements both good and bad. Many schoolmen are of the opinion that even the enlistment of the child in good enterprises because they are popular is bad for his education because it makes for mob-mindedness. On the other hand, we believe it is a fair question to ask: "To what extent has the public school the right to control the time and life of the child?" Our present tendency is to hand over to the state more and more of such direction on the ground that the state can do it more efficiently. The longer school day as at Gary, the increasing use of the summer vacation period for public school purposes, the calls for the creation of a department of education at Washington—all these and many others which we discussed in our opening chapter are indicative of a widespread and steady movement. We believe that the church *does* have a right to ask for a fair share of time in which it may do its educational work, although it must not ask the state to do that work for it.

INTERRELATION OF RELIGIOUS GROUPS

Another problem to be faced concerns the interrelation of the various religious groups. Many a promising week-day movement has been wrecked in the beginning and others have been seriously hampered because of mutual misunderstanding. There has been, it would seem, too much action taken on the basis that the public school is a Protestant school. Our Roman Catholic constituency have sometimes spoken the truth in referring to them in this fashion. We cannot stress too strongly the statement that the public school is a *public* school, and belongs to every citizen alike. It follows from this, therefore, that when such a movement as we are discussing is contemplated, every group and every individual must be taken into confidence from the very beginning. Roman Catholic, Jew,

Christian Scientist, and the members of every other faith, even the occasional agnostic, provided they are sincere, have the right to know and to voice any objections. Where cordial relations have been established between all concerned and no one feels that something has been "put over," plans made will meet with no obstacles. One of the valid objections raised by many public school men to the movement is based on the fact that the religious forces are divided among themselves.

There seems to be a growing sentiment among the Roman Catholics in favor of the week-day idea. It appeals especially to those of liberal tendencies and to those upon whom the additional parochial school burden rests heavily. Some of the higher officials are not willing to give up the parochial system for a week-day arrangement, but among the laity and the local clergy there is an increasing sympathy. The Jews are often opposed, or rather indifferent, because they are fairly satisfied with their present system of giving their religious teaching outside of public school hours. Recent signs of good-will and understanding between Christian and Jew, however, lead us to believe that the Jewish attitude is to become one of sympathy to the week-day school plan.

DESIRABLE TYPE OF SCHOOL

A problem which is related to the one we have just stated is the question as to the most desirable type of school to establish in a community. It seems that no one of the existing types in its present form will be ultimately satisfactory. On the one side, the denominational and loosely federated types have the advantages of freedom of teaching and of an easily correlated program for the local church. This is offset, however, by the tendency to narrow sectarianism and the wastefulness of divided effort. The closely federated, or so-called community type, and the non-denominational control type secure the advantages of cooperative effort and give a spirit of democracy to their teaching. But they are frequently found to be standing for a list of rather commonplace virtues which can be and are being taught in the public schools under the label not of religion but of morality, ethics and good citizenship. Then, too, it becomes practically impossible in connection with these latter types for the local church to plan and carry forward a unified religious education program. If we add to these considerations the fact that the movement ought to and undoubtedly will have the support of all religious groups, we can see that in any community, even as in Gary, there will be other schools in addition to the federated system.

The logical and, we believe, necessary outgrowth of all this will be a mixed type of organization which combines the general features of the second and third types. That is, there will be a loose federation of all the religious forces in the community to do the work which the overhead committees of the denominational-cooperating schools now perform. Under this loose federation, there will be both single schools and federated systems operating one or more schools under a single board. Even under the boards of these systems a choice of courses might be offered for the children of the same grade and development. Why should it be thought impossible in these days, when education is ceasing to mean indoctrination, that courses both conservative and liberal in character should be offered by the same central board, with the opportunity of selection by the parents and the scholars? In this way the advantage of democratic intermingling in such activities as worship, play and service may be preserved and, at the same time, each church which feels it has a distinct message will have the opportunity of proclaiming it. What will actually happen in each community in the matter of organization will depend upon the extent to which the churches are agreed in the aims and contents of their educational programs.

FOR FURTHER STUDY

COPE, HENRY F. *The Week-Day Church School.* Doran.

COPE, HENRY F. (editor) *Week-Day Religious Education,* pages 9-46; 69-91; 119-120; 124-136; 173-196. Doran.

LOTZ, HENRY P. *Current Week-Day Religious Education.* Chapters I-VIII, XI. Abingdon Press.

SHAVER, ERWIN L. "A Survey of Week-Day Religious Education," *Religious Education,* volume XVII, pages 83-120.

SQUIRES, WALTER A. *The Week-Day Church School.* Westminster Press.

YOUNG, THOMAS S. *Week-Day Church School Methods.* Judson Press.

See also reference list at conclusion of the following chapter.

Chapter Eight

A CHURCH SCHOOL FOR THE WEEK DAY
(*Concluded*)

Suitable Curriculum Materials

The question of organization leads most naturally into the problem of a satisfactory curriculum for week-day schools. If one were to commit himself as in favor of either one type of community organization or the other, it would not be quite so difficult to select material. But with the wide diversification of types

of schools and the differing needs of various communities and churches, it is not so easy. What has actually happened is that more and more both single schools and systems are using an eclectic curriculum and that, too, with a feeling that the particular choice of courses for any one year is more or less temporary and that a better selection will be made the next. As we have said, the more capable and progressive supervisors and teachers are planning their own courses.

It must also be apparent from our previous discussion of the nature of the curriculum of religious education that the choice of suitable materials for week-day schools is as difficult as for any phase of the total program. In the change which is taking place from an information or knowledge curriculum to that of a curriculum of conduct and character, one hears from local situations responses of many kinds. Sometimes it is a call for help, sometimes a warning not to disturb the nicely organized plans, sometimes a welcome note of progress—that a certain pupil-centered approach is meeting with success. The problem is further accentuated by the demands from some public school authorities that the curriculum be shown to them in black and white, that is, that the information-content to be mentally mastered by the pupil in the course of the year be definitely blueprinted for inspection. This is particularly true in those communities where the new emphasis upon the character aim in public education has not gained a place of equality with earlier aims of education for culture and for earning a living.

With reference to the coming curriculum for week-day schools, we venture two general predictions. One of these is to the effect that more and more the character and conduct aim will find expression in the choice of curriculum materials. One of the best advances in this direction is being made at Gary in spite of the difficult problems of finance, competition with the child's play period, the size of the school and the easy temptation to rest upon past laurels. The second prediction is made that we shall never have a standard and fixed curriculum for week-day schools. Not only will the courses vary in different communities but they will change from year to year within a single school or community.

THE QUALITY OF TEACHING

Another problem which deserves more attention than we can give to it here is that of the methods of teaching in week-day schools. From all we have been saying it will be clear that the successful week-day school must be taught in a way which views religious education as a dynamic, creative and functional process. We have described it as teaching in accordance with the project principle. The week-day school offers a real opportunity to break away from traditional methods and make the teaching of religion a fine art. A few have responded to the appeal; too many have not as yet.

If religious education is true to its name, the quality of its teaching should be at least on a level with that found in the public and private schools of the community. We say "at least"; it should surpass that teaching, for I am sure we believe, as religious education leaders, that the kind of education we stand for is more important than that offered by the secular school. This is true, not only where the latter views its task as primarily vocational but even in those schools where the central purpose is to make American citizens. This high standard is one of the objectives which week-day leaders must keep before them. It means that we must have our work in charge of the best trained leaders we can secure, whose equipment shall be measured not so much in terms of knowledge and the ability to impart knowledge as in terms of friendly fellowship with the boys and girls in their classes and in the ability to explain the meaning of life in accordance with the ideals and spirit of the Great Interpreter.

THE CORRELATION PROBLEM

One of the most difficult tasks which is involved in the week-day movement, as in other phases of the total church school program, is that of arriving at some form of desirable correlation. There should be a type of correlation by which the teacher of a week-day group gives a religious interpretation to the knowledge, skill and general experience gained by the pupils in school. But correlation in the sense of a complete unity of process with the program of the public school is neither possible nor desirable. Religion will always imply the revaluation of values; religious education will therefore mean a review of the facts and experiences of the secular school and of other activities of daily life in the light of the perfect ideal of the Kingdom of God. In a very necessary sense, there must be a kind of duplication.

But within the program of the church there is great need of correlation to prevent wasted effort. The week-day school is one more agency under church auspices and the church can ill afford to let it go on in competitive fashion with the hope that sooner or later the best agency will win out. We have had too much of this sort of thing; too many agencies, both within and without the church, have developed, each, to be sure, meeting some distinct need, but with little regard to the unity of the whole. Time is wasted,

money is spent uselessly, teachers misdirect their
efforts, and perhaps most important of all, the children
whom we would help become confused and lose interest.

The solution of this problem of correlation is not to
be found in any one patent remedy, nor will it be
accomplished shortly. Various procedures will have
to be tried out to discover the right direction to take.
Whatever success we shall have will come through the
solution of the three problems we have last discussed,
namely, through a more satisfactory type of week-day
school organization, through a more adequate curriculum and through the improvement of teaching
method.

EDUCATING THE COMMUNITY

One of the most serious obstacles to the success of
the week-day movement is to be found in the attitude
of many who appear to be most eager for its development. Like many another good idea, it is in danger
of suffering at the hands of the professional promoter.
Six years ago in surveying the movement, the writer
discovered six different agencies within one denomina-
tion seeking to adopt this baby Moses of the religious
education family, first discovered among the sand
dunes of Gary. Since that time, multitudes of religious education agencies, each with an institution to
maintain, have become ardent backers of week-day
schools. Some have gone so far as to maintain that
the Sunday school is a back number and that our only
hope lies in the newer institution. Those who have a

promotional viewpoint of this character are mainly concerned with establishing many schools, count succes in terms of the numbers of pupils who attend, view with pride this latest accessory to church machinery and measure results in terms of glib repetition of verses and meaningless busy work.

It need not be so. There is a better and more educational way to launch and carry on week-day work, which in the long run will be more effectual for religious education. The following suggestions are made upon the basis of the practical experience of a number of prominent workers:

1. No local community or church should be unduly influenced by outside or overhead agencies, but decide whether or not it should have a week-day school, after careful study and analysis of its local needs. It may be that the best interests of the total program of religious education will best be served in many communities by other means and agencies.

2. If it is decided that week-day schools should be instituted, the church constituency should be thoroughly educated, not only as to the desirability of having such an institution, but also as to the responsibilities that are involved and the problems which must be faced. There should be general sympathy with and understanding of the idea, not only on the part of the church forces but of a large number who are inclined to be indifferent. It is not wise to begin with a bare majority of the sentiment in favor; the entire community must be committed to the idea.

3. The financial costs of the new enterprise must be considered and plans made for adequate support. If the movement is to be of value in raising the level of religious education, it must do a *better* piece of work than the average Sunday school. It is not enough merely to do more of the same type of work that has characterized that institution. Trained teachers must be employed; adequate equipment must be provided; high grade curriculum materials must be purchased. The financing of a week-day school system is therefore a genuine test of whether we really believe in religious education.

4. By all means one must avoid doubtful arrangements to use the buildings, equipment, teachers, or other facilities of the public schools. Although there may be communities where no objections will be raised, such organic relations compromise the principle of separation of church and state and in general bring the movement into disrepute. Even the matter of giving public school credit, especially in the grammar grades, is open to question. Likewise, legal entanglements and disputes between religious groups are to be shunned.

5. A modest beginning should be made rather than an attempt to start the movement on a large scale. A few grades only the first year, or the establishment of one or two centers as an experiment, is a good plan. These can then be carried on with regard to quality of work and a high standard set for future development. At the same time, weaknesses can be studied and corrected.

6. It is sometimes necessary and advisable to prove the worth of the week-day plan by establishing schools which meet outside of public school time. As has been implied earlier in the discussion, it is not to be assumed that the granting of public school time is the major factor in making a week-day school a success; it is rather the kind of activity which is carried on which enlists the interest and energies of the pupils, regardless of whether the school is held on released time or outside public school hours. It is much better to have the public school authorities see a demonstration of high grade religious education and then share their time with the churches than to give time on the basis of promises and regret it afterward.

7. The primary responsibility for the establishment, maintenance and supervision of week-day schools should be in the hands of the churches of the community. Interested individuals organized apart from church control or extra-church agencies cannot carry on week-day schools meeting the standards we have laid down.

8. A thorough system of expert supervision should be maintained. This is essential to insure, not only the best grade of equipment and materials, but especially to see that the teaching is of a high order and that constant improvement is being made. Money spent for a skilled and experienced supervisor is one of the best investments week-day schools can make.

THE KEY PROBLEM

Practically all that we have been saying reveals the fact that the outstanding problem of the week-day movement is that of carrying forward a program of religious education on a high level, rather on a *higher* level than any previous agency. If it can do this, many of the problems we have been discussing will be practically solved. One denominational leader says: "While legal opposition has slowed up the movement, it has given us an opportunity to insist upon better standards. It was for the demonstration of these better standards that I went into the business of establishing demonstration schools. Wherever this has been done, those schools are recognized among the leaders as sustaining standards of which the public school can approve and have resulted in a wide interest in the local parishes on the part of both the church-school children and the adult members of the church." Says another leader who has charge of the week-day work in an eastern state: "We are going to be very careful about getting schools established until we know what is going to be done as to high quality and that we can be proud of the results." This, then, is our key problem—to develop a school of religion which is truly religious and truly educational to a higher degree than ever before.

CONTRIBUTIONS OF THE WEEK-DAY MOVEMENT

Now that we have suggested how some of the problems involved in the week-day movement should be met, we may well conclude our discussion with a summary of its positive contributions. To begin with, it has been a most powerful factor in emphasizing the need of religious education. The general public have been stirred in the past few years by this earnest attempt to develop a school of religious training as they have not been for generations. The need of religion as a factor in the education of every child, the need of using the educational approach in teaching religion, the demand for more religious education than the spasmodic efforts on Sunday, and the insistence upon a superior type of training than has previously been carried on—all these have been given great prominence through the rise of the week-day school.

Teaching religion on the week-day has reminded us that religion is not to be viewed as a segment of life, associated only with Sunday clothes and a sacred building. The very fact that it is now being taught in a new setting and correlated, however poorly, with public school and play experiences, has tended to give the child a new value for religion, its value for every day life.

The week-day school, being a new institution, has offered opportunities for new methods and experiments which the traditional Sunday school could never have initiated. Some Sunday schools, to be sure, are progressing, but the many favorable factors associated with the newer institution have made progress possible on a larger scale. It is to be hoped that crystallization will not set in, but that this experimental attitude will continue for a long time to come.

While the question of the aims of religious education has been by no means fully settled, it is safe to
say that the week-day movement has done much to
aid in a clearer understanding of its ultimate and
immediate objectives. The many discussions which
have been held in promotional gatherings, in meetings
of curriculum committees, in editorial rooms and in
general conferences of students of religious education
have all aided to bring new light to professional and
lay leader alike. We are more sure than a decade
ago that religious education must fit the child for daily
living and that the full meaning of the term education
is not to be found in a process of intellectual instruction only.

In the week-day school we have had a new emphasis upon the use of standard physical equipment, especially in such items as libraries, furniture, room decora-
tion, heating, lighting, and ventilation, which show
the influence of the public school. Although most
week-day schools have not yet attained anything like
perfection, the advance is most encouraging.

The movement has likewise spurred the curriculum
makers to produce new and generally improved
courses. These courses could never have been introduced in such wholesale fashion into Sunday schools.
Even though some of the rather hastily prepared materials now used as week-day courses will have to be
discarded, it is significant that the week-day session
is frequently viewed as the activity session of the
larger church program and as such has required
courses in which Christian living is emphasized.

In this new school we find a greater stress laid upon courses of a practical nature. Missions, social service and the problems of everyday living are at the center of the curriculum in many week-day schools rather than being viewed as "not having much to do with religion" as they have been in so many Sunday schools.

We have said that the week-day school had its origin in the desire to have a real school. It has therefore aided greatly in the improvement of teaching methods. Although there is a large percentage of week-day schools which are little better than Sunday schools in the character of their teaching, there is a growing number that are pointing the way to a higher level.

A correlative contribution is the stimulation which has been given to training for leadership. The week-day school leaders have insisted that they must have trained teachers and thousands are now being prepared for this work. The dignity and worth of the teaching ministry is once more coming to be recognized.

As we have also stated, one of the problems to be faced is that of the correlation of programs. While from one standpoint the week-day school has added one more agency to the already confusing number, its wide-spread development has brought leaders to see the imperativeness of facing the problem squarely. The number of agencies which can efficiently help the child seems to have reached the saturation point and, rather than settle the matter by wasteful competition, movements are now under way to unify the program.

We can thank the week-day movement for hastening the day of cooperation.

Similarly, the week-day school has greatly aided the movement for more united and cooperative effort among Protestant churches. It has brought them together in a common enterprise and caused them to lay aside their differences of creed for the sake of their children. While few would care to see a single Protestant church with a uniform creed and organization, most of us would like to find a common unity of spirit, within which there could be diversity of thought and method. The week-day school has sown the seeds in the lives of the coming generation and the harvest will be reaped.

A very significant effect, which we must recognize and credit to the movement for week-day religious education in part, is the awakening of public school leaders to the necessity of giving character education a far larger place than it has heretofore had in the public school program. Scarcely a meeting is held in the interests of secular education, either local or national in importance, but that the subject is up for discussion. Most of our larger cities are at work upon character-education programs and syllabi.

The development of a self-mastering and altruistic personality, of a righteous and victorious character, is not to be thought of as an exclusive goal of education. It is rather an inclusive goal toward which all other phases in education should make their contributions, and by which the standards of all other goals are to be judged. This necessity for permeating all the work of the public school with character ideals is undoubtedly the subject to which leaders in general education are giving, and for some time will continue to give, their largest thought.

Even though the advocates of week-day religious education may not feel that the week-day movement has in every instance been a direct success, they can rejoice that their cause has aided in bringing about this counter reconstruction from within. But even when this reconstruction shall have been more completely effected, there will still remain to the church-school leaders the task of educating their pupils to live upon a plane which no public employee may advocate, because the latter's character goal is set by vote of men, and the former's by the internal authority of a God-given conscience.

We can predict the future of the week-day movement only in a general way. That it will remain a separate and distinct agency, somewhat apart from the church, is doubtful. But that its work will abide and that the values which we have pointed out will be conserved in the enlarged and enriched program of religious education we are definitely assured.

FOR FURTHER STUDY

COPE, HENRY F. (editor) *Week-Day Religious Education,* pages 46-68; 92-119; 120-124; 136-172. Doran.

FORSYTH, NATHANIEL F. *The Organization and Administration of Week-Day Church Schools.* (In Preparation.) Abingdon Press.

Gove, F. S. *Religious Education on Public School Time.* Harvard University Press.

Hauser, C. A. *Latent Religious Resources in Public Education.* Heidelberg Press.

Lotz, Henry P. *Current Week-Day Religious Education.* Chapters IX, X, XII. Abingdon Press.

Shaver, Erwin L. "A Survey of Week-Day Religious Education," *Religious Education,* volume XVII, pages 120-142.

Shaver, Erwin L. in *The Teaching Work of the Church* (a symposium) Chapter VIII. Association Press.

"Week-Day Religious Education" (a symposium) *The International Journal of Religious Education,* volume I, number 6 (March, 1925).

See also reference list at conclusion of the preceding chapter.

CHAPTER NINE

A CHURCH SCHOOL FOR THE SUMMER VACATION

One of the most interesting developments in religious education in recent years is the daily vacation Bible school, or as it is becoming more frequently and more accurately known, the vacation church school. About a generation ago the first schools were set up in downtown churches in the larger cities to care for children whose only occupation was to play in the crowded streets. The churches, usually empty at this season of the year, were thrown open to provide an attractive program of play, craftwork and instruction in the Bible. College students home on vacation were recruited to do the teaching. Since that time many changes have taken place in the nature of the program and in the teaching personnel. The movement has extended beyond the downtown, home-missionary type of church and is being viewed as quite a necessary agency for almost any kind of church or community.

This movement for a session of the church school during the summer vacation has won increasing recognition because of many factors, some of which we are to treat in this chapter. It seems to the writer that this interesting agency has unique possibilities,

even exceeding those of the regular Sunday session
of the church school or the movement for week-day
religious education which we have just been discussing.   It is our purpose to point out the nature of some
of these possibilities in the interest of making advances
in our total program of religious education.

Advantages Due to the Time Factor

A large portion of the advantages of the vacation
school over other agencies of religious education lies
in the fact that it is held just when it is, in the vacation period.   From this fact there arise a number of
distinct advantages upon which we shall comment.

Actually there is less competition with the many
other agencies and institutions set up to help the child
interpret his life religiously.   Without disparaging
any of the well-intentioned efforts to help develop
character in our children and youth, we must say that
our present increasing duplication of effort is having
a decidedly bad effect upon the child himself.   It is a
wonder that some of our research groups have not
before this turned their search-lights upon what a child
really thinks about all the energy that is being spent
to make him good.   During the regular work and
school year we so drive ourselves and our children,
that it is perhaps necessary to go away where these
things are out of sight and out of mind, even organized religion.   But the vacation school is unique in
this fact of its freedom from competition, for no one
seems to be physically and mentally able to do much

by the time June has come. The vacation school, at least so far, has things its own way, if it takes advantage of the opening which is thus afforded. It must be on its guard, however, for there are several agencies with jealous eye upon the summer period. The public school leaders are thinking and talking about pre-empting these months for a continuation of the work of the year. The programs of "achievement clubs" and summer camps are making inroads into this frontier time.

The vacation school, meeting for a period of from two-and-a-half to three hours a day for four to six weeks, gives the time needed for an all round experience, which is so vital for character development. The school becomes an actual social unit in which the members work and play, study and worship together. In contrast with the efforts of other agencies, such as the Sunday school and the week-day school, there is an overwhelming advantage in this fact. Whenever one urges teachers and leaders in these institutions to enrich their programs with something other than pre-cept giving and cold mental digestion (or rather indigestion) of theories about how to live, he meets with the almost universal answer: "We have so little time; we must teach them at least the more important things about life." As though teaching consisted in or could be accomplished through an intellectual process solely! And as though, granting the importance of intellectual development, it should take first place and these other things may be dispensed with as rather tag-end experiences! But the vacation school offers the time to carry on a rich and thoroughly integrated program of cooperative Christian living. With many weaknesses, doubtless, but nevertheless with earnest effort, it has seen this opportunity and is reaching for its fulfillment.

We must add to this fact of allowing an amount of time, equal to in practically every case and in many cases double that of the Sunday school, the fact that this time is so distributed that it insures educational results. An examination of the laws of learning applied to memorizing, to the development of attitudes of reverence and the like, and to the formation of habits in general, would lead one to say that in the vacation-school program we have, perhaps not ideal conditions, but nevertheless highly desirable conditions in our favor.

Turning from the matter of more time to an examination of the nature of that time, we at once become aware of the fact that the summer is the playtime of modern society. Careful reflection as to the ultimate purpose of religious education should lead us to see that civilization must be taught to play. Our leisure time is increasing. But, unfortunately, since that leisure time is being made possible by an age of marvelous machinery and highly organized and competitive industry, we have carried over into the leisure periods the spirit of work and commerce. "Spectatoritis," the spirit of the fan who takes his play by proxy, the entrance of the commercial motive so strongly into all forms of recreation, the rapid growth of professionalism, and other unhappy consequences have come upon us. Is there not need for us to learn the true nature of play and to teach our children to find in play activities not *wreck*-reation, but *re*-creation of body, of mind, and of spirit? The vacation school can do this as no other institution because of its peculiar time of meeting.

Carrying still further our discussion of the spirit of play, we note also that the play attitude is the desirable atmosphere in which real learning takes place. One is tempted to enlarge upon this fact at some length. Suffice it to say that interest and effort go hand in hand, and when we say this we do not ignore the fact that the discipline of overcoming difficulties is developed through the interest in an objective farther removed, but nevertheless one which the pursuer wants because he likes it. Even the forefathers endured religion here below because it promised a heaven of everlasting bliss, where they could play for the eternities. We should like to give examples of vacation school projects entered upon in the play spirit which gave birth, not only to some definite contribution of service for the Kingdom of God, but to its inseparable twin, a forward step in character for the server. But we must not be tempted; every vacation school worker is familiar with them. Our point is that the vacation school has as its invincible ally the spirit of play without which educational method would be barren indeed.

The summer brings to the fore the out-of-doors life. Some vacation schools have taken advantage of this fact and planned activities outside of the classroom for their pupils, although in too many cases these activities have not been intended as having very definite character-building value, but are rather viewed as rewards for attendance upon the more important activities of study and worship. The out-of-doors, however, has values of its own, very tangible values, too often forgotten in this age of formal religion. Have we forgotten that religion seems more natural under the open sky than in crowded buildings? Have we forgotten that the three greatest religions of the world, Mohammedanism, Judaism, and Christianity, were all born and nurtured in an out-of-doors country and seem to have suffered somewhat when taken inside, because the lakes and the mountains, the sun and the stars, the trees and the fields are shut from view? Have we forgotten that God has revealed in nature without his great laws of the beginning and the growth of living things and that there are the pictures of the earth as he made it, majestic, beautiful, and of endless variety in its natural, unspoiled state? What an opportunity, after the seclusion of the winter, if we take advantage of it! And so the vacation school can actually bring its pupils face to face with the God of the open air in real, vivid and lasting experiences in which definite lessons are taught much more easily than the Sunday or week-day sessions of the remainder of the year can impress them.

TURNING LIABILITIES INTO ASSETS

There are a number of factors which militate against the successful organization and administration of a vacation school of religion. At least these are always raised as objections by those who want nothing of the sort carried on. Let us examine these liabilities and see if they are entirely on the debit side of the ledger.

The pupils are just out of school and are tired of studying. To some extent this is true. The mechanization, necessary or unnecessary, in most of our day schools for the nine or ten months of the year does produce in many boys and girls a distaste for anything that smacks of the schoolroom. But it is interesting that it does not take long for them to yearn for it again. To expect a child to find plenty to do, after a rich supply of activities provided for him throughout most of the day has suddenly ceased, is expecting too much. If our general education were more enlightened, perhaps it would enable a child to go on of his own accord and create outlets for his powers. There are a few schools which do just this. But the average one does not, and we therefore find Johnnie and Mary begging father, or more likely mother, for "something to do," unless father or mother has packed them off to a summer camp or has driven them into the street, there to mingle with the "hoi polloi" and catch their ideals and habits of a doubtful value.

The opportunity of the vacation school lies just at this point. Its best chance lies in capitalizing this desire for something to do, something to do which is not viewed in the spirit of mechanized drudgery, but rather in the spirit of creative expression. It is not to duplicate the points of emphasis at which the public school is weak but to catch the spirit of public school method at its best, which is the point of departure for a worth while vacation school. Not formal recitations, and books, and straight lines, and unbroken routine; but happy and informal groupings, with challenging enterprises calling forth originality and initiative, with the emphasis away from selfish inversion, and lessons being learned continually although unconsciously.

Few churches have any definite plans for the summer. Even those which have vacation schools do not often correlate the program provided with the Sunday session for the summer or with the work which the church has been trying to do educationally during the months past. It is just a good thing to have, and so it is established and often forgotten by the constituency. The general let-down of the summer causes the church-school officials to worry through until Rally Day brings new life. In all this the vacation school suffers, except as it is manned and carried on by a small but faithful group who see its possibilities.

In this fact of general indifference, however, there is one consolation. One can have a new and a different program. Think of the things which have taken place in the name of religious education in a vacation school, which, had they been a part of a Sunday school program, would have been taboo, not alone from the fact that they were held on Sunday, but as well from the fact that the things done were so "secular." In the absence of any very definite summer plans and with the necessity of building a program from the ground up, the director and teachers of a vacation school have a real asset.

While it is true that many vacation schools do reach a large number of children not touched by the church during the year, it is becoming less true that the movement is a missionary agency. The vacation school is now being adopted by the self-sustaining church to care for its own children. But in view of the nature of the summer season, as we have indicated, the attendance of the children who are in the Sunday school the remainder of the year is relatively smaller. Some are away on vacations at the shore or in the mountains. Others, encouraged by this fact and the example of their parents, take a "stay-at-home" vacation. All of which makes interest in a vacation school somewhat difficult, were there not other powers of attraction.

But this fact of smaller numbers is not without its advantages. The residue of the faithful come from a real desire; they are in a certain sense a select group. One then has *ecclesiola in ecclesia,* a church within a church, which by its leavening power may work a new life in the larger body when the fall comes. One can do things with this little group which would not be possible with greater numbers, even as Jesus wrought more effectively when he turned his attention from the multitudes to the intensive training of the twelve.

In carrying on a vacation school one must regroup the pupils, both because new pupils are enrolled who were not in the Sunday school, because many who were in Sunday school classes do not come, and because of the general nature of a vacation school program. This may be viewed by some as involving difficulties and raising problems, but it should also be viewed as a thing to be desired. One would not want to hold up close gradation on the basis of age or public school advancement as an ideal for a school of the Christian life, in which a wide variety of activities are being carried on. The very fact that both Sunday-school and public-school groupings are not possible, makes an opening for new groupings, those in which a new criterion may be set up; namely, interest in common enterprises and ability to take part in carrying them through. This basis of grading is particularly adaptable to vacation schools with their emphasis upon play, worship, handwork, and other projects, as well as upon study.

One of the difficulties which often stands in the way of the establishment and successful carrying on of a vacation school is that of obtaining rooms and equipment of a suitable character. This is met in many cases by distributing various grades in different churches, where the school is an interdenominational affair. But since a vacation school does other things, more like the activities of everyday life, an abundance of raw materials and tools is needed, and churches sometimes find this an obstacle. However, once a school is held the supplies will be obtained. It may be said in passing that the acquisition of raw materials suggests an opportunity both for hearty cooperation of adults in furnishing things which they can easily give and for the resourcefulness and thrift of the children in discovering that much can be done with the articles ordinarily sent to the scrap heap. From this standpoint the need and apparent lack are real blessings in disguise. From another standpoint, the success of a vacation school in overcoming the handicap paves the way for securing better space, equipment, and materials for the sessions of the church school during the year.

The vacation school requires specialists in various types of activity as those agencies which emphasize instruction do not. This makes a difficulty as do the facts just discussed. There is need for someone who can lead play on a Christian level. Teachers of drawing, basketry, and other forms of handicraft are needed. The leading of worship assumes the proportion of a real art, which requires more skill than leading "opening exercises." These various activities of the program require a church to hire persons who are thus skilled or to conscript them from its membership. But when the need has been met, in whatever way, the church begins to see that there is more to character training than giving good advice and need for the talents of many leaders other than those of a preacher or an instructor in the narrower sense of that term. Such a view of religious education opens the way for the use of many persons among the church membership, who might be called "associate teachers," each of whom at the proper time and place should give himself or herself in friendly fellowship to the growing children and youth in the church circle. The possibilities of an enriched view of teaching in the sphere of Christian character development are thus seen and the vacation school may lead the way, if it chooses.

CONDITIONS OF SUCCESS

In the concluding section of this discussion we wish to set forth some of the conditions which should be met by a vacation school in order to guarantee success.

In the first place it is necessary that vacation school leaders keep the right goal of forming habits and developing character, which we have stated as one of the relatively unique opportunities afforded to this religious education agency. With the advantages we have enumerated there should be little excuse for "short-circuiting" the process of character development, by giving undue emphasis to the intellectual side of the program to the exclusion of other activities we have mentioned, or by their relegation to a secondary place. Let the entire program be planned and carried through so that the experiences afforded actually train the children to think, work, play, and worship as citizens in the Kingdom of God.

One of the dangers which confronts the vacation school as well as other agencies of religious education is the temptation to do the work, through the aid of a few professionally trained and paid specialists, which ought to be shared by the parents and the members of the church at large. It is all very well to say, as many do, "The home no longer teaches religion. Therefore, we, the vacation school, or the Sunday school, or the week-day school, must do that task." This is well intentioned and justifiable as a remedy in an emergency situation. But neither the vacation school nor any other agency working in and for a Christian society, which believes in the home as the fundamental training unit for that society and the church as a family upon a larger scale, should limit its program in this way. It is not doing its best work, unless it is definitely helping to train the parents to resume their rightful function as teachers of righteousness and likewise helping to train adult church members similarly to give themselves in helping the children in their midst live as Christians. The vacation school must proceed earnestly to carry on its program in such fashion as to do these things and not attempt character education by proxy.

One should not have to urge vacation school leaders to keep their training goal on a high Christian level. But, because of the early history of some vacation schools and the growing popularity of the movement, we fear that sometimes vacation schools limit their aim and efforts to making moral Americans, that is, Americans who obey the laws and adopt the existing community code of morality which is practiced around them, instead of looking higher to the ideals set by the principles of the Kingdom of God. While the vacation school may rightly do Americanization work, it should do that work on the Christian level, so that the "patriot's dream" of the pupils is not that of the America that now is, but of the America that is to be, when her "alabaster cities gleam, undimmed by human tears."

It will be well for the vacation school that it preserve and refine the missionary spirit in which it was founded. The Christian world has less and less use for the condescending spirit in missions. It surely cannot be said that the first vacation schools, in which college students with the spirit of service went forth to do mission work in the slums of our cities, were taught by those of condescending spirit. But some benevolent patrons have tended to look at the school in this light, which has hampered its development as a school for every child in the church parish. The new spirit of missions must prevail, the spirit of mutuality in giving and receiving," the spirit of world friendship and brotherhood. In this we believe the vacation school will do its just share.

Although not quite so youthful as the movement for religious education on the week-day, the vacation school is sufficiently young to be classed as in its plastic age. It is to be hoped that it will not too soon become set and cease to grow, or that it should ever come to that condition. It has shown evidences, fortunately, that it can adjust itself to new conditions and make improvements as they are found to be acceptable to religious educators. The vacation school should, just now especially, when changes in method and curriculum are taking place with such rapidity, keep itself open to the best procedures. It can do more; it can, because of the favorable factors we have indicated, do its full share in experimentation and discovery of these procedures.

Without doubt, one of the things which must be done to make the vacation school a lasting success is to integrate it with the total program of religious education. We trust, however, that, before this takes place, or as a condition of its taking place, its distinctive contributions to religious education in the week-day and Sunday sessions of the church school will be thoroughly recognized. Those unique possibilities which we have pointed out in the earlier portion of the discussion, must not be lost in the closer relationship which should rightfully exist between all agencies for Christian character training.

FOR FURTHER STUDY

ARMENTROUT, J. S. *Administering the Vacation Church School.* Westminster Press.

GAGE, ALBERT H. *How to Conduct a Church Vacation School.* Judson Press.

IKENBERRY, CHARLES S. *The Daily Vacation Church School.* Brethren Publishing Co.

KNAPP, E. C. *The Community Daily Vacation Bible School.* Revell.

KRUMBINE, MILES H. *A Summer Program for the Church School.* University of Chicago Press.

STAFFORD, HAZEL S. *The Vacation Religious Day School.* Abingdon Press.

STOUT, JOHN E. and THOMPSON, JAMES V. *Organization and Administration of the Daily Vacation Church School.* Abingdon Press.

See also leaflets, manuals, handbooks and curriculum materials published by the various denominations.

CHAPTER TEN

FORWARD STEPS IN TRAINING LEADERS

The entire trend of our discussions in the preceding chapters should by this time have focussed the reader's thought upon one outstanding need, that of a leadership which will be able to carry through the program for the present day as we have pictured it in the new approach to method, in the changing curriculum and in the new agencies of teaching found in week-day and vacation church schools. To move forward to the higher levels of religious education which we have been urging without more efficient leaders than we have had in the past is as impossible as for us to expect to maintain a high quality of public and private education on the standards for selecting teachers which prevailed a generation ago. The trained leader is the key factor in the progress we hope to make. Trained leaders we must have.

It is not the purpose of this final chapter to go into detail as to the various qualities which describe the teacher of religion who can cope with the present-day problems of childhood and youth. We are to concern ourselves rather with the steps which ought to be taken and are being taken to develop such leaders. Before proceeding further, however, we wish to make one statement of caution as to the place of the professionally trained and paid educational leaders, who are more and more to fill the responsible positions in various portions of our church educational programs. If, as we have pointed out in the opening chapter, we are to free religious education as well as general education from the dangers of institutionalism, we must avoid shifting the entire responsibility for Christian training to a few professional workers. We must have these and will have them in larger numbers in our coming program, but instead of their being employed to reduce the amount of time and thought which the lay worker in the church gives to training children in religion, their employment should result in an increased amount of lay service given for this purpose. The trained specialist is to be, not a substitute for the less trained volunteer lay leader, but an inspirer, a demonstrator and trainer, and an organizer of religiously educative experiences for pupils which require the fellowship of many parents and adults. Provided we can thus multiply the efficiency of our present willing lay leadership by securing such specialists and do not refuse as parents and adult members of the church to associate ourselves with growing childhood and youth in the experiences of service, study, play and worship in the church life, we can then conscientiously bring into our midst an increasing number of professionally trained and paid leaders. We thus have need for better trained specialists who are professionals and also for better trained lay leaders. All that we say in the following pages applies to both groups.

BETTER TRAINING METHODS REQUIRED

Previous to the last decade the emphasis in leadership training was largely upon popularizing the idea. This earlier period of convincing the church of the need for training its educational leaders has been followed by a period marked by the organizational emphasis. The machinery has been set up and a program developed. System has replaced unorganized spurts in local churches. Independence has given way to cooperation in local and continent-wide enterprises. We are now launched upon a definite policy and have perfected the organization to carry it on.

At the present time, however, there is a growing feeling that the time has come for a forward step in the improvement of method in the training process. Up to the present time we have carried on a book- and information-centered program. The teacher has been considered fitted for his work because he has assimilated the subject matter of a prescribed number of books covering Bible content, rules of teaching procedure and related themes. We are still in the position of the earlier public normal schools, a position away from which they have been moving steadily for some years. We must find ways of enriching our present theoretical study of how to be a leader in the church school so that the training process becomes a living experience and actually fits the teacher to *do* his work more effectively. In the treatment of the theme of our chapter we shall seek to do four things, namely: (a) to set up in brief fashion a statement of what would seem to be a more ideal method of training than we now have, both for those leaders who are to be professional specialists and for the lay teachers; (b) to suggest how the time honored workers' meeting in the average church may be reconstructed to produce more valid training results; (c) to describe some of the changes which are now taking place in the curriculum of training conducted cooperatively by the Protestant churches; and (d) to state the plans now under way for the development of new and improved training curricula.

TRAINING THROUGH SUPERVISED ACTIVITIES

A more ideal type of training, involving the supervision of the leader as he is actually engaged in leadership responsibilities, implies two facts. In the first place, it suggests that he shall have, or be given, a definite opportunity to work at the task in which he is seeking to develop skill. That is, he shall learn by first hand experience just how to proceed. In more popular parlance, he is to have "practice work" or "laboratory work" as well as a study of theory. In the second place, the implication is that these leadership projects are to be supervised in order that educational values shall accrue to the one in training. He is to be so guided in his leadership responsibilities that he steadily but surely comes to perform them better and thus grows in control of leadership skills.

It should be added also that these practice tasks should be real tasks. They may be simple at first, but ought to be a part of the actual and practical program of religious education as it is carried on in the local church or community. In no other way can there be "carry on" into the tasks assumed after the more formal training period is over.

After all, there is nothing startlingly new in this proposal. It is the characteristic procedure of training leaders in the general education field, as we have noted. It is the avowed policy of our more successful business concerns to take men with a good general educational background (not an early, "rule-of-thumb," theoretical specialization in a school), and place them in shops and offices to work their way up quickly to their positions by having the underlying experiences at first hand. A number of our best directors of religious education are relying more and more upon the personal and individual guidance which they can give their teachers than upon formal courses of training. Our theological seminaries are opening their curricula to courses of this practical nature. The few experiments in conducting training classes based upon the actual and immediate problems of the members of the group have demonstrated the soundness of the principle.

ELEMENTS IN SUCH A PROGRAM

One who believes in this better training method must provide for two elements in his program. The members who are to be enrolled in the training group must have or be assigned definite responsibilities for leadership. Just what positions each one should have is to be determined by a number of factors, such as his natural capacities, his need for developing the skills in which he is deficient, the positions of leadership needed by the church, the opportunities available for practice work, and others.

In surveying the field of opportunities we note such as these: class teaching in the Sunday, week-day or vacation sessions of the church school as a regular, apprentice or substitute teacher—especially the latter two in the case of young and inexperienced leaders; planning and leading services of worship; directing programs of recreation at socials, on camping trips and hikes; initiating and guiding a wide variety of service projects, as in missionary and social service education; the special types of leadership such as directing pageants or plays; story-telling; leading in music; and acting as a department officer or committee member.

The student in training must have, as he accepts and carries on these activities, a clear purpose of making them the means of developing his powers of leader-ship. He must constantly take the attitude of the experimenter. He will first analyze his situation and define the problems he finds, then after conference with the training group leader make a plan for trying out some suggestion for improvement, give it a fair and conscientious trial for a period of time and meas-ure its results. All the time he must keep before him his ideal of how he would like to have the work go and move patiently and steadily forward until he succeeds.

A second element in training leaders through such activities is that of supervision. It is necessary to have the students in training actually at work on tasks of leadership, but it is equally necessary, if we wish something more than a too wasteful "trial-and-error" way of learning, to guide them as they discover and face their responsibilities. This means a program of supervision, looking after the leaders, visiting them in their work, observing their points of strength and weakness, organizing critical and helpful reports upon what has been observed, and suggesting how changes may be made to improve the work. The leader of the training group must be in constant touch with every member and give a large amount of personal attention to their work, if he is to really help them in it.

The conferences which this general supervisor of the training work holds with the students in training may be either or both of two types. One is the personal conference, in which much can be said and done which is impossible in a larger group meeting. The best supervision will always make large use of this intimate contact between supervisor and the one in training. Another type is a meeting of those in training by small groups or as a single body. Here each one in turn will present his problems, his plans for solving them, his successes and failures in trying out the plans and ask for help and guidance from the other members and from the supervisor. In many cases the supervisor will have an organized report to make.   As a result of these mutual conferences new ideas and plans will be developed and encouragement given to try them out.   Then before the next meeting, these are put into execution and further reports made as to how they have worked.   Such a conference for those in training will partake of the spirit and purpose of the customary teachers' meeting, but should be more carefully and systematically conducted so as to eliminate its weaknesses.

How to Go About It

If a church is convinced that this way of training leaders is sound and practical, we suggest that it proceed as follows:

First, secure the understanding and consent of the teachers who are to take the training.   The value of such an approach as this will be largely lost unless its purpose and method are thoroughly comprehended. Teachers must be willing to pay the price of training in terms of hard and patient work and in terms of willingness to give new ideas a fair trial.   They must be willing to become disciples and learn from each other and from the supervisor who leads the group.   Therefore, if any church looks forward to using this kind of training procedure, it must prepare the way, not only as far as the members of the training group are concerned, but also in the case of the church members, for many of them will be more or less affected by the activities carried on.

Second, a competent supervisor must be secured. Sometimes more than one may be used, each specializing upon certain departments of the school or types of work. This person may or may not be a director of religious education. Sometimes a public school supervisor or teacher is available; at other times a specialist in religious education problems is located near and may be secured for part time service in supervision. Or perhaps one of the local teachers who has been taking special training may be selected.

A word might also be said in passing about the spirit of a good supervisor. No one will be fit to do this important and difficult type of work in a church school who depends upon the fact of his official position. He must win his way into the hearts of those whom he is set to help. He is not an executive officer to say "Do this" or "Do that," but a friendly co-teacher with experience and willingness to help. He must possess sympathy, tactfulness, patience, cordiality and similar traits on the one hand, while on the other he must keep his vision of ideals in church-school teaching and exercise perseverance in attaining them.

At this point we must give one note of warning. Provide every opportunity for the supervisor to do actual supervising. Do not let him be an assistant to the janitor, to the pastor or to the superintendent. Relieve him of administrative and other details so that he can be present in the groups where the religious education process is being carried on. Let him give his best energy and thought to this one thing. His task is not to do the work of others for them, but to help them do their work better.

Third, when these two steps have been taken, the church should then set up a program of training. This is to be done, as we have indicated, by systematically selecting the members of the training group, providing each one with a leadership responsibility which is appropriate and then arranging for supervision and reports upon visits made. The frequency and character of these will depend upon such factors as the size of the group, the number of meetings held, the time the supervisor has to give, and the like.

Here is a challenge to our churches to pioneer in a new and a better type of leadership training. To those which try, there will come decided improvement in their programs of work and a corps of leaders ready to face and to solve each new problem as it arises.

Training Values of Teachers' Meetings

It has not been customary to think of a teachers' meeting as the time to train church-school workers. This process has been thought of as taking place only in those definitely organized classes pursuing certain units of the Standard or other types of training courses. However, we are turning our attention to the teachers' meeting as a form of training with real possibilities. There are two general reasons. In the first place, a great many teachers do not avail themselves of the opportunities of an organized training school or class. For these there must be provided a place of training and, since most of them do attend the regular teachers' meeting, it may be made to help them. In the second place, the constant improvement of training methods has caused us to see that the teachers' meeting offers many possibilities for educational growth that we have overlooked in the past.

From among a number of reasons why we may class the teachers' meeting as a training opportunity we may point out four, which are, however, closely interrelated. First, it has a practical objective, namely —to discuss and carry into execution definite plans for making the school more efficient. Second, there results from this fact an interest manifested both in willingness to attend, to take part in the discussion and to work on committees. Third, most of the plans made in the meetings of the business type are put into fairly immediate use. Fourth, the members of the teachers' group in such meetings work together in making and carrying out plans. Every one of these foregoing facts suggests educationally valuable training, if advantage is taken of them, for teachers are going to make improvement in their teaching powers in proportion as they are interested in their work, see some practical outcome of their efforts, put their ideas to a speedy trial and multiply information and skill by cooperation and division of labor. These are principles of sound educational theory.

Unfortunately, teachers' meetings are not always conducted with a consciousness of these educational aims. The superintendent, or other person in charge of the meetings, does little or no planning for them. Consequently the discussion wanders hither and thither. All the many difficulties which the school and its staff face are brought one after another into the limelight at each meeting, are pessimistically discussed and passed by. There is little real fact information brought to bear upon them from authoritative books or from the experience of other schools. If an outside specialist is asked to speak, it is too often with the purpose of hearing an interesting address rather than seeking his help with a definite problem. The meeting usually closes with no plans made and no controlled trial of any of the suggestions which may have been put forward. Such are the weaknesses which have kept teachers' meetings from giving the real training which they should be able to give.

How, then, should one proceed to make the teachers' meeting a real training experience and avoid these obstacles to success? We may offer the following general suggestions:

1. The entire year's series of meetings should be carefully planned with the needs of the school and the teachers in mind. The goal should be to make some definite improvement in the local teaching methods. The various problems to be taken up may be determined at the first meeting of the teachers and a tentative schedule of topics made for the year. This should not be taken as an inflexible program, however, for many things may happen which will necessitate a change in the interests of the best work.

2. If one were thinking of these topics or problems as the chapter headings in a text, he might thus say that the text of the series of meetings is to be one's own school. This will ensure lively interest, keep the meetings practical and make it easier to apply the ideas brought forward. Therefore, be sure to keep the school's real and immediate needs in mind in selecting the topics for the year.

3. It is much better to take up a few problems one at a time than to attempt to solve all the difficulties one has all at once. It might even be advisable to take up only one problem in a year and to get somewhere with it. Then the teachers would become encouraged and also learn the method of systematically facing the next problems they take up. It is, of course, possible that some schools with a larger number of teachers may be undertaking to solve several problems at the same time, provided committees are actually at work between meetings studying and trying out each one of the plans agreed upon.

4. Careful preparation should be made for every meeting. The theme (problem in one's own school) should be definitely stated in terms that every teacher can understand. Then the program committee, including the leaders of the meeting, should have a step-by-step plan for taking it up. In this plan there should be a large place given to finding out just what experts in the field recommend doing and just how other schools have faced the same problem. This means careful book study and either visits to or correspond-

ence with these places. A teachers' meeting will not get far with any problem for which advance preparation of this kind has not been made.

5. With the problem carefully stated and this definite information introduced, the meeting should then be prepared for profitable discussion. The leader must be careful to enlist the ideas of all without letting a few do all the talking. He should also keep the discussion focussed upon the central theme.

6. Out of the discussion there should come some definite conclusions and a plan of action which can reasonably be expected to be put into operation right away. One or more committees should be appointed to undertake the necessary work.

7. At the next session the first item of business should be a report from these committees. Sometimes the plans made may be put into execution in the time between two sessions; in other cases it may require a much longer period to give them a fair trial. But a report at each session with the necessary discussion of the progress made and possible revision of plans is a good thing.

In addition to basing teachers' meetings upon problems such as these, which might include how to prepare a lesson, how to conduct a worship service, how to choose a course, how to use the Bible, what kind of equipment to have, etc., there are other ways of giving the teachers' meeting a training value. For example, individual meetings may be devoted to reviews of books or magazine articles, planning for special days, coaching in the use of certain typical lesson materials, demonstrations of certain techniques of teaching, a parent-teachers' meeting, an annual banquet or the reports of delegates to conferences or of visitors to other schools.

In any case, however, those who plan and conduct the meetings should bear in mind the foregoing suggestions in order to ensure the real training values which we have sought to point out. If this is done, we shall have strengthened our total training program and reconstructed a time-honored church-school agency for a period of renewed usefulness in the building of the Kingdom.

IMPROVING THE PRESENT TRAINING CURRICULUM

The steady advance in method and the improvement of the curriculum of religious education in general are manifest in the field of leadership training to a degree commensurate with its importance to the total program. During the past few years there has been a systematic effort on the part of those in charge of both denominational and interdenominational programs to make changes for the better in what is known as the Standard Leadership Curriculum. A few of these improvements may be noted.

1. Formerly the curriculum consisted of eight general units, all of them required—four to be taken the first year and four the second—and four specialization units, all required, to be taken the third year. At the present time six general and three specialization

units are required, leaving three units to be taken as electives. This larger freedom of election has resulted in an increased popularity for the course because it more appropriately meets the needs of local churches and individual teachers and officers.

2. This principle of election has resulted in there being added to the curriculum a large number of units covering not only specialized types of work such as dramatization and pageantry, missionary education, recreational leadership, week-day and vacation schools, but also more units of Bible study. This enrichment of the field in which one may elect training has obvious values.

3. It may safely be said that at the present time the quality of work being done compares favorably with that carried on in our colleges and normal schools. While there is the same range in quality that one notes in these institutions throughout the country because of differences in the ability of pupils and of standards in different localities, the changes that have been wrought in the past few years warrant the belief that it should not be difficult to maintain the Standard Curriculum approximately on this level.

4. As a result of years of experience, the principles and methods of administration have been developed to a point of great efficiency in the face of opposition at certain points on the part of those who were some-what reluctant to apply strict educational standards to the religious education field or who were naturally inclined to be slack in these matters. The rapid

growth of interest in the course on the part of local churches and communities as shown by the figures of four years past is a testimony to the wisdom of insisting upon thoroughgoing standards in training leaders who are to serve in such a high calling as Christian education.

5. Ever since the course was initiated, the texts used have shown an advance in quality and quantity of content. A few persons have been tempted to refer to them as "repetitious pocket manuals." Some of them have frankly deserved the implied slight. But this is scarcely a fair appraisal today, because of certain changes that have taken place. Most of the denominations, and certainly the International Council, provide for a choice from a number of approved texts for the several units. In the list one finds the very latest volumes produced by the creative thinking of the most advanced workers in the field. In the International list the book of the private writer and publisher stands on a par with those offered by denominational houses. Because of the increase in the number and size of pages recommended by the Teacher Training Publishing Association for its texts and the type of authors it has been selecting to prepare them, we are seeing produced through this agency books that any college professor might well be proud to use in his courses.

6. Just now the Standard Leadership Curriculum is on the verge of the most significant change it has yet been through—that of ceasing to be a text-book

course and becoming an experience-centered course. While actual practice is as yet somewhat removed from this ideal objective which its administrators are holding for it, it must be said that there are certain facts which point in this direction. Instead of treating the units of the course as being limited to the study of one text, they are more and more being taught in such a way that a far richer experience is provided for the pupil in training. Many approved instructors are building their own syllabi and using a wide variety of reference books; certain of the specialization and elective units, in fact, can be given only on the basis of an approved syllabus; and in many of the schools which extend over a longer period than a single week, a wide variety of reference reading, observation, and occasionally practice, is required. The time would seem to be not very far distant when, instead of using single text-books for the units of this curriculum, they will be taught in accordance with a general syllabus adaptable to local needs and to the initiative of individual instructors, so as to provide for a more nearly first-hand and thorough training experience.

7. Two other indications of improvement are also to be found. One is the establishment of a few laboratory schools for practice work, which promises to become an established portion of the training curriculum where conditions are favorable. The other is noted in experiments whereby the teaching of certain units has been based upon the actual problems of the local schools and their teachers, discovered by the

training class leader through observation and investigation before the course began.[1]

NEW TRAINING CURRICULA

For some time it has been felt that the training program has not only needed an improved method, but that it ought to be extended to care for three groups of leaders not now benefited by the Standard Curriculum.   In the first group are a great many leaders who have completed the work of the Standard Curriculum and, having begun the practice of improving their skill as teachers, want to go on.   Another group consists of a considerable body of professional workers who wish to keep in touch with the rapid advances now being made in method and curriculum. For these two groups it is now proposed to build an Advanced Curriculum which shall compare favorably both in scope and quality with the work now being done in professional schools of religious education.

Those who are interested in leadership training have also observed that leadership does not come by accident, but that if we want a sufficient number to give themselves to teaching service in the Christian church, we must begin early to select and train them.   Hence the inauguration of a leadership curriculum for a third group, the future leaders, who are to be found among young people of middle adolescent age and experience.

[1] See article entitled "Laboratory Foundations of Leadership Training" by H. Shelton Smith in *Religious Education*, vol. XXII, pp. 37-40.

This High School Leadership Curriculum has been experimented with for the past two years and is now to be included in the total program of training.[1]

Perhaps the most significant fact about these two new leadership curricula is not so much that they set up an extension of the range of training opportunities available as that they offer a chance for incorporating into the procedure of training leaders the theory of method which we have discussed in the early portion of this chapter. This is possible because these curricula are being built from the ground up and are free from the encumbering traditions as to method which have acompanied our use of a book-centered course in the past. The central feature in method emphasized in the use of these curricula is the actual experience of working at the task in which one is seeking to improve his skill. In addition to this fundamental approach of "learning by doing," there are utilized many other educational principles of the character we have set forth in this volume. We believe we are warranted in saying that the type of method now incorporated in these two new curricula of leadership training will set a standard for the improvement of method in every segment of the total program of Christian education.

[1]Those interested in the High School and Advanced Leadership Curricula should send for descriptive bulletins issued by the International Council of Religious Education, 5 South Wabash Avenue, Chicago, Illinois.

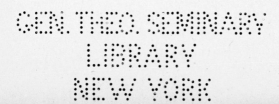

FOR FURTHER STUDY

ATHEARN, WALTER S. *The Indiana Survey,* volume I, chapters XII-XVI. Doran.

BARCLAY, WADE C. *Training for Leadership and Teaching.* Abingdon Press.

CAVERT, SAMUEL M. *Securing Christian Leaders for Tomorrow.* Doran.

COPE, HENRY F. *Organizing the Church School.* Chapters VI and VII. Doran.

KLYVER, FAYE H. *The Supervision of Student-Teachers in Religious Education.* Teachers College.

SHAVER, ERWIN L. *Programs for Teachers' Meetings.* Pilgrim Press.

SHAVER, ERWIN L. *Teaching Adolescents in the Church School* (A Teacher Training Planbook). Doran.

SMITH, H. SHELTON. "Laboratory Foundations of Leadership Training." *Religious Education,* volume XXII, pages 37-40.

STOUT, JOHN E. *Organization and Administration of Religious Education.* Chapters VIII and IX. Abingdon Press.

WEIGLE, LUTHER A. et al. *The Teaching Work of the Church,* pages 34, 44, 56-59, 167-170, 193-194, 204. Association Press.